TAXING VISIONS

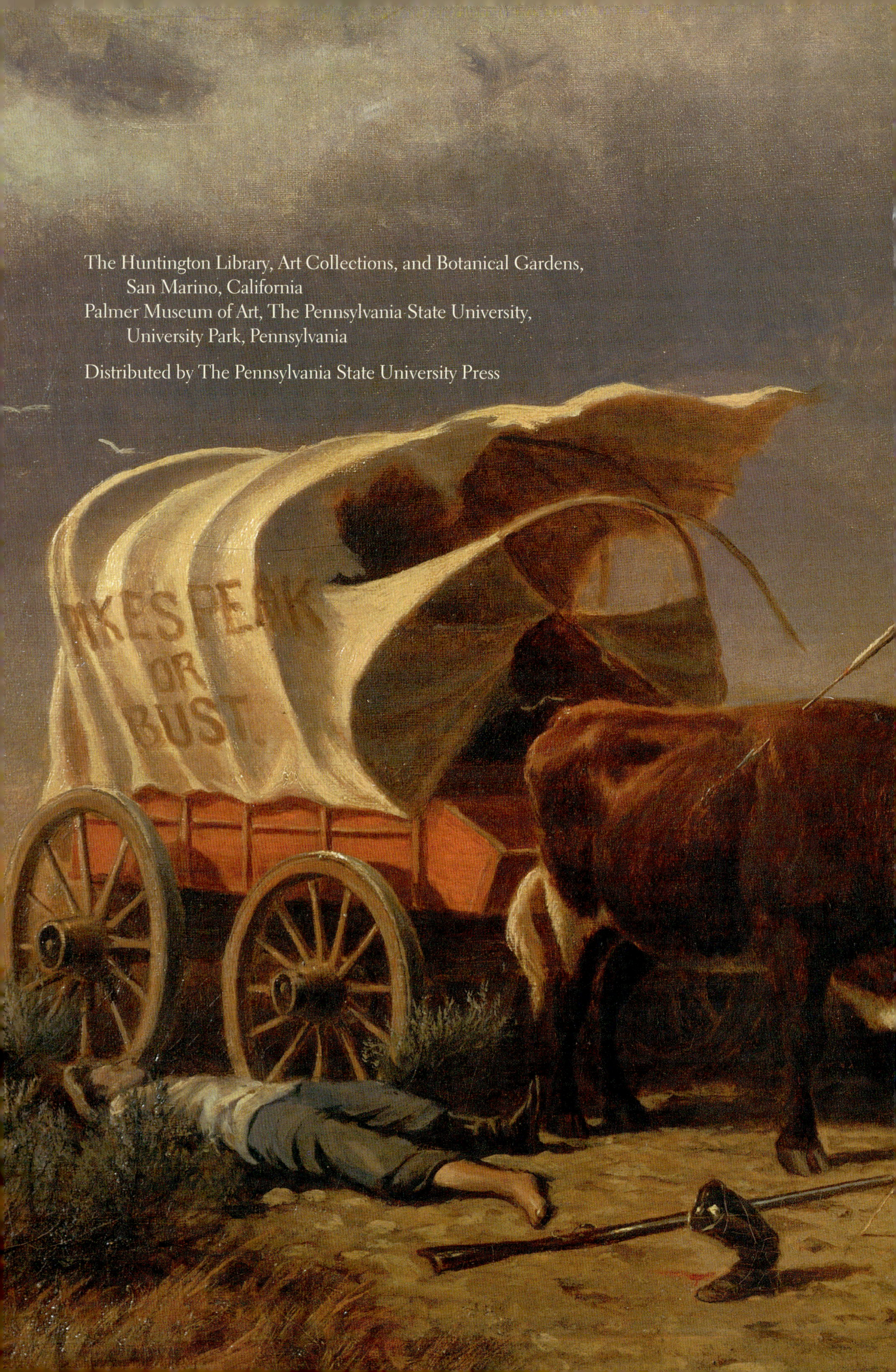

The Huntington Library, Art Collections, and Botanical Gardens,
San Marino, California
Palmer Museum of Art, The Pennsylvania State University,
University Park, Pennsylvania

Distributed by The Pennsylvania State University Press

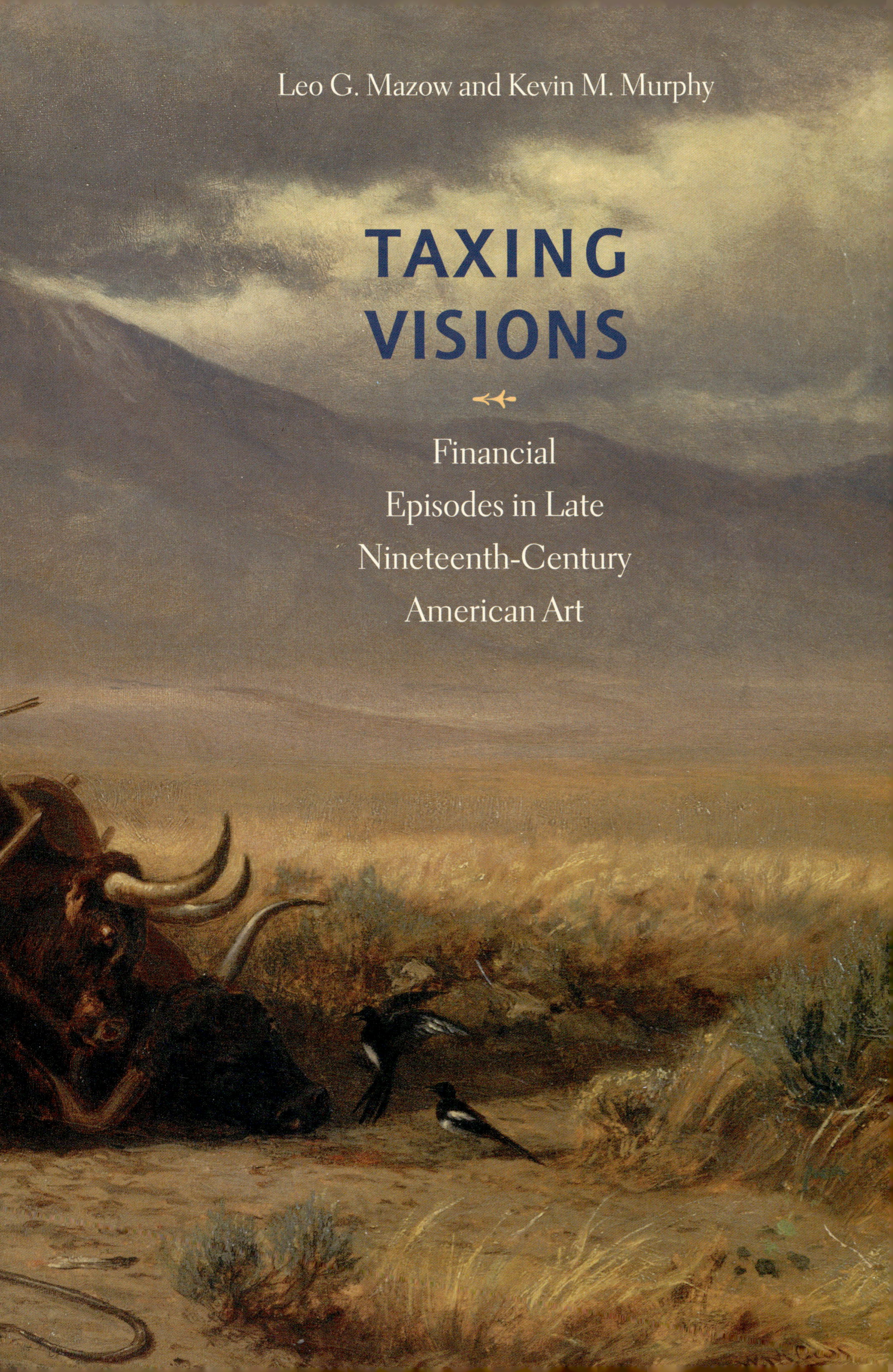

Leo G. Mazow and Kevin M. Murphy

TAXING VISIONS

Financial Episodes in Late Nineteenth-Century American Art

Published in conjunction with the exhibition *Taxing Visions: Financial Episodes in Late Nineteenth-Century American Art*, held at The Palmer Museum of Art, The Pennsylvania State University, September 28–December 19, 2010; and The Huntington Library, Art Collections, and Botanical Gardens, January 29–May 30, 2011

Printed in China
Designed by Jennifer Norton

ISBN 9870911209686
U.Ed. ARC 10-107
Library of Congress Control Number: 2009943976

Cover illustrations: (front) Alfred Kappes, *Tattered and Torn*, 1886, oil on canvas, 40 × 32 inches. Smith College Museum of Art, Northampton, Massachusetts. Purchased with the Beatrice Oenslager Chace, class of 1928, Fund, the Rita Rich Fraad, class of 1927, Fund for American Art, the Kathleen Compton Sherrerd, class of 1954, Fund for American Art, and with restricted acquisition funds; (back) Victor Dubreuil, *The Cross of Gold*, ca. 1896, oil on canvas, 14 × 12 inches. Private collection. Courtesy of Berry-Hill Galleries, New York.

Opposite: Julian Alden Weir, *The Flower Seller*, ca. 1879, oil on canvas, 40⅜ × 22⅛ inches. Brooklyn Museum. Gift of George A. Hearn, 11.522. Detail of fig. 31.

Title page illustration: William de la Montaigne Cary, *Pikes Peak's or Bust*, early 1870s, oil on canvas, 21 × 36 inches. Hood Museum of Art, Dartmouth College. Purchased through the Guernsey Center Moore 1904 Memorial Fund. Detail of fig. 43.

Opposite table of contents: Frank Moss, *A Difficult Job*, n.d., oil on walnut panel, 8⅝ × 7⅛ inches. The State Museum of Pennsylvania, Harrisburg. Transfer from Hope Lodge, 75.1. Detail of fig. 27.

Penn State is committed to affirmative action, equal opportunity, and the diversity of its workforce.

This project is supported in part by an award from the National Endowment for the Arts.

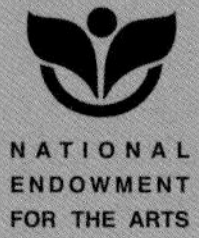

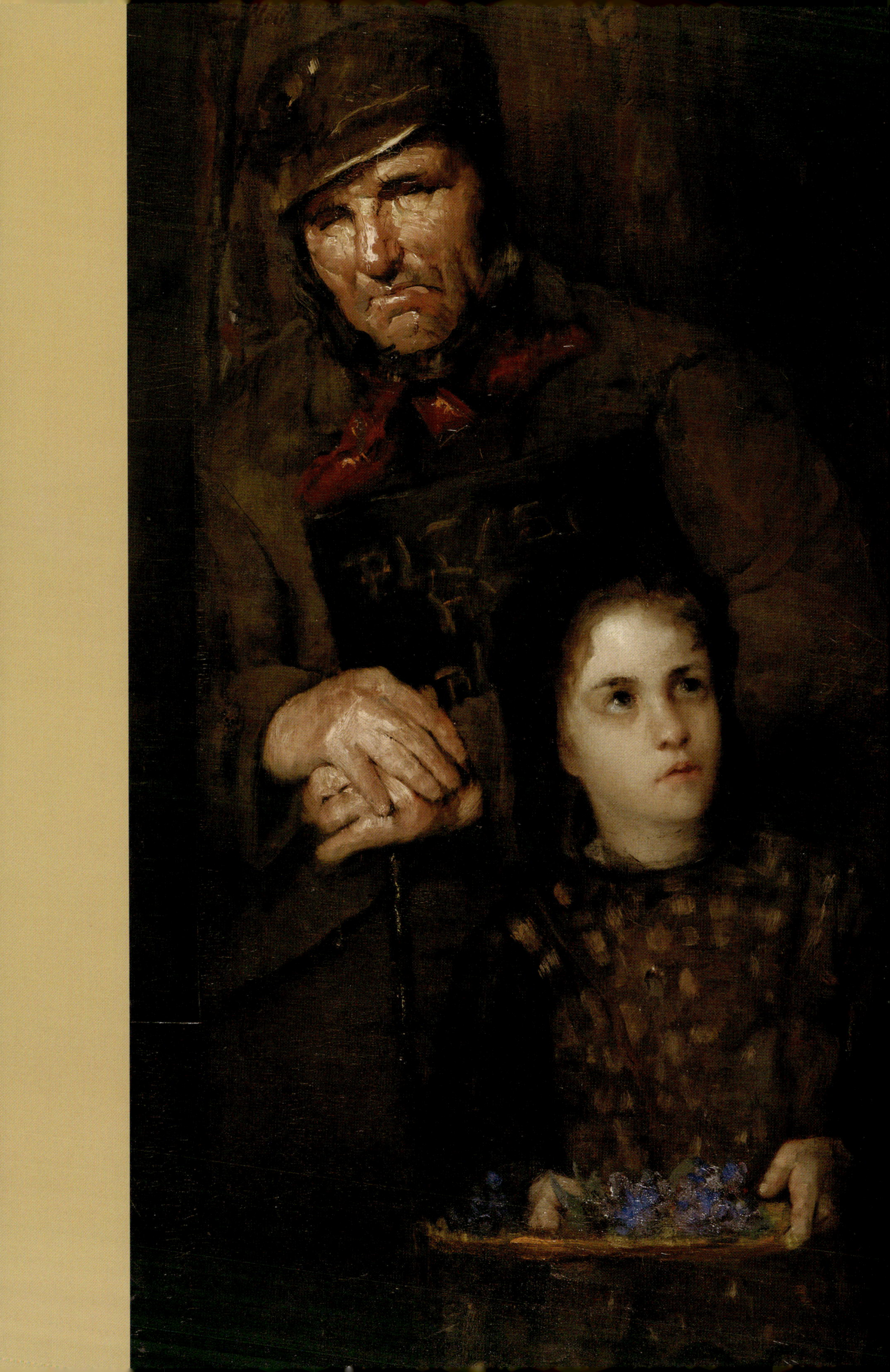

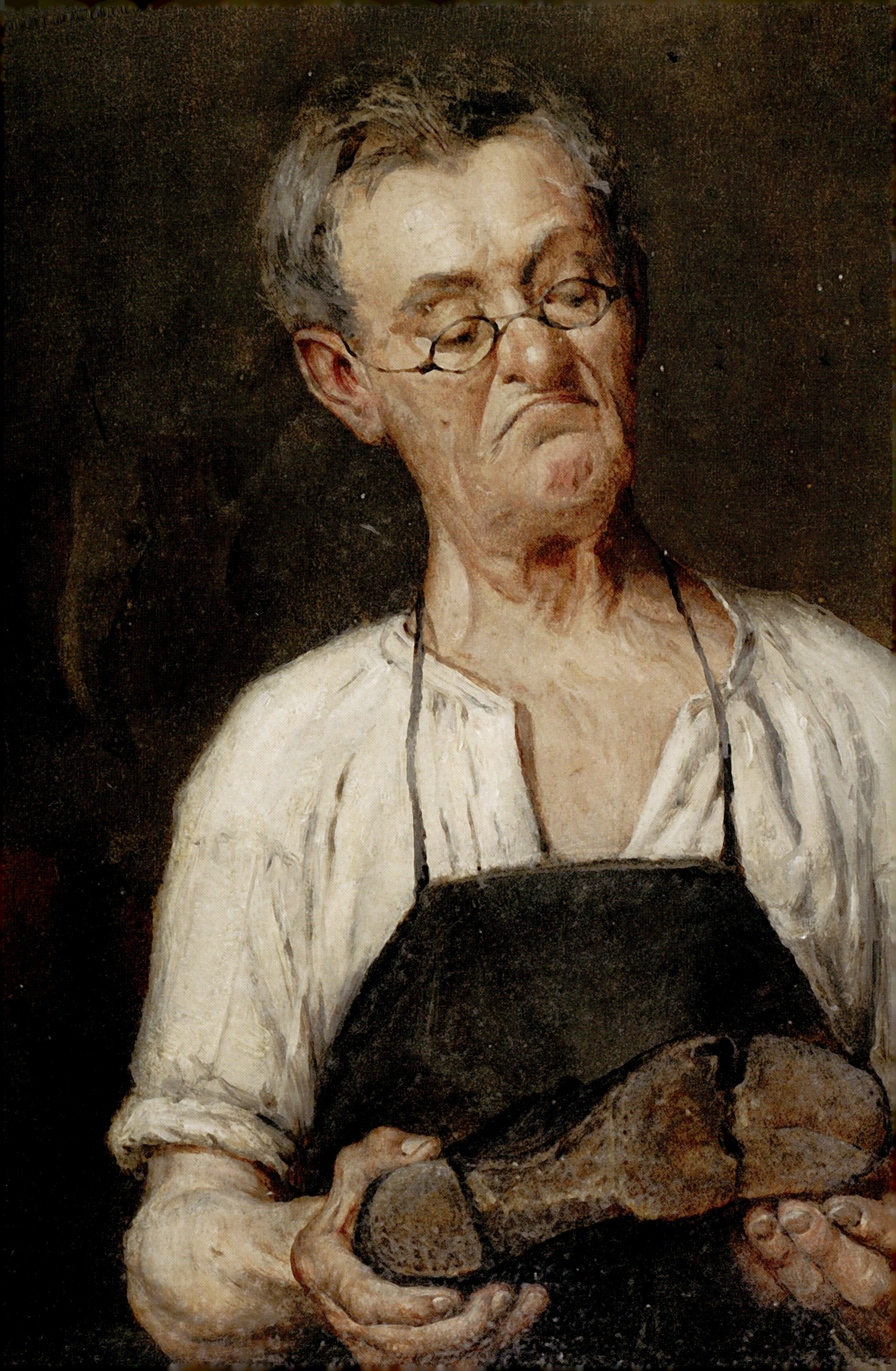

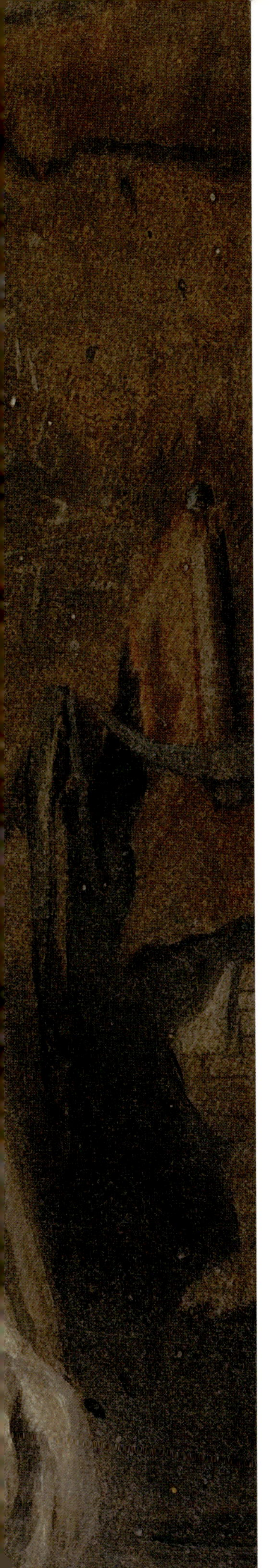

Contents

Lenders to the Exhibition

Brandywine River Museum, Chadds Ford, Pennsylvania

Brigham Young University Museum of Art, Provo, Utah

Brooklyn Museum

Cincinnati Art Museum

Colby College Museum of Art, Waterville, Maine

Mr. and Mrs. Thomas Davies

Delaware Art Museum, Wilmington

Fine Arts Museums of San Francisco

Garzoli Gallery, San Rafael, California

Georgia Museum of Art, University of Georgia

Hood Museum of Art, Dartmouth College, Hanover, New Hampshire

The Huntington Library, Art Collections, and Botanical Gardens, San Marino, California

Indianapolis Museum of Art

Herbert F. Johnson Museum of Art, Cornell University, Ithaca, New York

The Long Island Museum of American Art, History & Carriages, Stony Brook, New York

Montclair Art Museum, New Jersey

Morris Museum of Art, Augusta, Georgia

Museum of the City of New York

New-York Historical Society

North Carolina Museum of Art, Raleigh

Palmer Museum of Art, The Pennsylvania State University, University Park, Pennsylvania

The Pennsylvania State University Libraries, University Park, Pennsylvania

Princeton University Art Museum, Princeton, New Jersey

Private collection, courtesy of Berry-Hill Galleries, New York

Reynolda House Museum of American Art, Winston-Salem, North Carolina

Smith College Museum of Art, Northampton, Massachusetts

Jean and Alvin Snowiss

Spanierman Gallery, LLC

State Museum of Pennsylvania, Harrisburg

Terra Foundation for American Art, Chicago

T. W. Wood Gallery and Arts Center, Montpelier, Vermont

Acknowledgments

Taxing Visions: Financial Episodes in Late Nineteenth-Century American Art had its genesis in a chapter in Leo Mazow's doctoral dissertation on George Inness (1996), in which he analyzed the painter's engagements with reformer-journalist Henry George's so-called Single Tax. Mazow published that chapter as a separate article in 2004 and hoped one day to examine the manner in which financial hardship played out more generally in the work of Inness's contemporaries. Kevin Murphy, meanwhile, was writing a dissertation doing just that, as well as examining several components of the marketing and patronage—the "business"—of American art in the late nineteenth century. His article of 2002 on Winslow Homer's promotional and professional practices in an evolving corporate economy emerged from his work on his dissertation (2005). In *Taxing Visions*, Mazow and Murphy return to their investigations of the intersection of art and social and economic forces at a turning point in the nation's history. In this exhibition and its accompanying publication, they propose to bring their scholarly interest in this neglected field before the wider public. The ambiguity of the term "taxing" in the exhibition's title is obviously deliberate; it refers both to the imposition of taxes, tariffs, and other levies and to those images that, precisely because of the subject matter of financial hardship, "tax" our sensibilities. Ironically (if cruelly), the economic situation took a turn for the worse in the early stages of preparing this exhibition, and the topic became especially timely. We are therefore all the more grateful to those who are making the exhibition possible financially at this difficult time.

Taxing Visions is supported at the Palmer Museum of Art through generous grants from the Suzanne H. Arnold Charitable Fund; the George Dewey and Mary K. Krumrine Endowment at the Pennsylvania State University; and the National Endowment for the Arts. The Palmer venue is also supported by the Friends of the Palmer Museum of Art.

At the Huntington, the exhibition and catalogue have been supported through a generous gift from Steve Martin. An endowment from Susan and Stephen Chandler also provides funds to support exhibitions in the Virginia Steele Scott Galleries of American Art.

In addition, we express deep gratitude to the institutions and private collectors who have agreed to lend works of art to the exhibition. We greatly appreciate their ready understanding of the intellectual program of the project, and their willingness to part with key works from their own galleries for an extended period of time. At the Palmer Museum of Art and the Pennsylvania State University, the following individuals have generously offered their time, insights, encouragement, and expertise: William Doan, Associate Dean for Administration, Research, and Graduate Studies, College of Arts and Architecture; Dana Carlisle Kletchka, Curator of Education; Greg Kordas, Assistant Registrar; Sandra Stelts, Special Collections, Penn State University Libraries; Henry Pisciotta, Penn State University Libraries; Beverly Balger Sutley, Registrar; Craig Zabel, Head, Department of Art History; Tess Kutasz, Katherine Staab, Stephanie Swindle, former graduate assistants; and Jennifer Cozad, Elizabeth Warner, and Barbara Weaver, the front office staff at the Palmer. We extend our thanks to Jennifer Norton for her expert design work. We also thank the members of the *Taxing Visions* Advisory Committee at Penn State for their time, insights, and assistance. Finally, deep gratitude is extended to graduate assistant Cali Buckley, who handled the photography and rights and reproductions requests for this publication with uncommon grace and efficiency.

At the Huntington, *Taxing Visions* has benefitted from the calm competence of Gregg Bayne, Exhibits Manager; Elizabeth Clingerman, Assistant to the Director of the Art Collections; Jacqueline Dugas, Registrar for Exhibitions; Nicole Goetting, former Curatorial Assistant; Sydney Moritz-Levine, Rights and Reproductions Assistant; Christian Mounger, Graphic Designer; Pat Pickett, Exhibits Preparator; and Jessica Todd Smith, Virginia Steele Scott Chief Curator of American Art. We acknowledge with gratitude the invaluable research assistance of Tia A. Vasiliou, Graduate Curatorial Intern. Finally, the present catalogue has benefitted from the expert copyediting of Susan Green and Jean Patterson.

We would like to thank the following individuals for answering research queries and facilitating loans: George Adams and Maya Fineberg, George Adams Gallery; Joan Adler, Straus Historical Society; Carma de Jong Anderson; Julie Aronson, Cincinnati Art Museum; Christine Berry, Spanierman Gallery LLC; Teresa Carbone, Brooklyn Museum; Enrique Chagoya, Stanford University; John Coffey, North Carolina Museum of Art; Thomas Davies; Meredith Davis, Ramopo College; John Driscoll, Babcock Galleries; Lee Glazer, Freer Gallery of Art/Arthur M. Sackler Gallery, Smithsonian Institution; William Eiland and Paul Manoguerra, Georgia Museum of Art, University of Georgia; Eleanor Jones Harvey and William Truettner, Smithsonian American Art Museum; Betsy Kennedy, Terra Foundation for American Art; Amy Kurtz Lansing, Florence Griswold Museum; Joyce

Mandeville, T. W. Wood Gallery and Arts Center; Linda Muehlig, Smith College Museum of Art; Kimberly Orcutt, New-York Historical Society; Clarence Burton Sheffield Jr., Rochester Institute of Technology; Jean and Alvin Snowiss; N. Lee Stevens, State Museum of Pennsylvania; and Marian Wardle, Brigham Young University Museum of Art.

As many nonprofit organizations have learned, collaborations, where tasks and limited resources are shared, have become a necessity. Although the Palmer Museum of Art and the Huntington Art Collections are 2,250 miles apart, we have enjoyed this productive and collegial enterprise. We hope that the diverse audiences we reach at our locations and through this publication will equally benefit from this exciting project.

Jan Keene Muhlert
Director
Palmer Museum of Art
The Pennsylvania State University

John Murdoch
Hannah and Russel Kully Director of the
Huntington Art Collections

Introduction

LEO G. MAZOW AND KEVIN M. MURPHY

Taxing Visions: Financial Episodes in Late Nineteenth-Century American Art explores the subject matter of taxes, rent, economic depression, and financial inequity in a group of visually provocative paintings and works on paper. Alongside the period's leisure-filled Impressionist landscapes, bountiful still-life paintings, and class-conscious portraits, practitioners working in a variety of stylistic idioms also reckoned with the financial panics and individual hardship that marked the Reconstruction, Gilded Age, and early Progressive eras. The paintings, drawings, and prints in this focused exhibition demonstrate the experience of economic downturn with occasionally startling clarity, in some cases picking up where facts, figures, and the printed word leave off. Through satire and protest, artists have confronted recession and depression with equal parts reportage, invective, humor, and hope.

American art between 1860 and 1900 registers a heightened sensitivity to financial hardship. Given the precarious economy, artists could not help but address troubling financial issues. Severe panics and depressions paralyzed the nation in 1857, 1869, 1873, and 1893; crippling deflation after the Civil War, leading to political debates over the gold standard, also affected more individuals than is often realized. The period also witnessed the rise of large, technologically advanced businesses that changed the nature of commerce and employment while ushering in modern consumer culture. The unprecedented scale of immigration, urbanization, and industrialization laid bare class distinctions and disparities between labor and capital as never before.[1] Artists in turn faced not only economic uncertainty but also increasing competition at home and from abroad, with dramatic shifts among cultural institutions and patrons. A number of the artists represented in *Taxing Visions* lived on the margins of their profession, never quite reaping the rewards of their peers who successfully navigated the institutions that emerged after 1860 to exhibit and sell American art.[2] Indeed, artists who chose to depict the failures of the capitalist system—often as thinly veiled allegories of their own pecuniary trials—may have found their work unwanted, especially when juxtaposed with placid Tonalist and Impressionist landscape paintings.

Figure 1
William Sidney Mount, *Fair Exchange, No Robbery*, 1865, oil on panel, 26 x 33½ inches. The Long Island Museum of American Art, History & Carriages, Stony Brook, New York. Gift of Mr. and Mrs. Ward Melville.
IN EXHIBITION

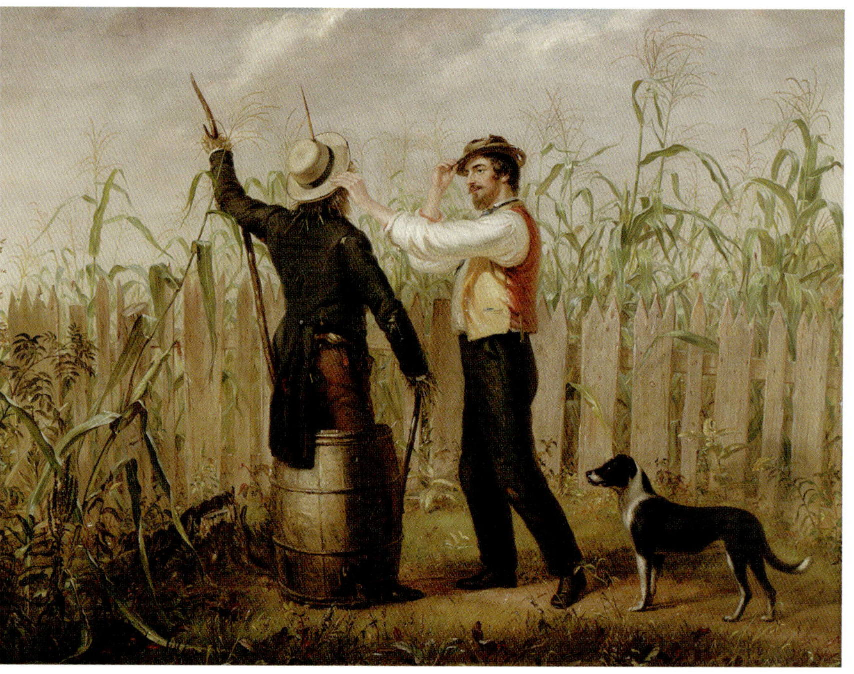

Many of the artists in this exhibition (John George Brown, Henry Mosler, Louis Moeller, among others) depicted financial ruin using academically informed linear styles and polished surfaces. This sentimental gloss and apparent verisimilitude sometimes offset the threat of the subject matter (surely, for some artists, unintentionally). A few artists, such as James McNeill Whistler, Albert Pinkham Ryder, and George Inness, contributed to and were informed by the more modernist facture of Impressionism and Tonalism. However, they used this gambit in much the same way as those artists who used academic polish to mitigate their subject; they simply resorted to another, more au courant, mode of dissembling through style.

This exhibition, by focusing on the last forty years of the nineteenth century, calls to mind uncannily similar intersections of art and money at the beginning of the twenty-first century. Today's audiences are far from alone in experiencing market busts, foreclosures, unemployment, underemployment, ruined family fortunes, foiled business plans, and the racial, ethnic, and geographic tensions with which these calamities are so often intertwined. The coping strategies of the past thus provide a lens for the economically beleaguered present.

In organizing the exhibition, we make no claims for its inclusiveness—though we do wish we could have examined more narratives or "financial episodes" than we do here. Several of the works we had in mind were unavailable for loan or reproduction, which impeded our scope and, for better or worse, dictated some of our parameters. Moreover, due to the present economy, *Taxing Visions* has turned into a smaller and somewhat different project from the one we conceived of five years ago. Focusing more incisively on the works that are featured and reproduced ultimately proved fruitful, however, which was an unexpected result of reconceiving the project as a "focus exhibition." As we examined the works through multiple methodologies—both traditional and less orthodox—we found that several of them operate on many levels. As socioeconomic critiques, they require explanation and interpretive "breathing room," unlike a cavalcade of greatest hits designed to overwhelm by the visceral power of sheer numbers and formal sumptuousness. Our more intimate approach suggests that even those subjects that appear straightforward—such as child laborers and starving artists—often symbolize much larger anxieties that pervaded American culture; the "surface" subjects are often stand-ins for other players.

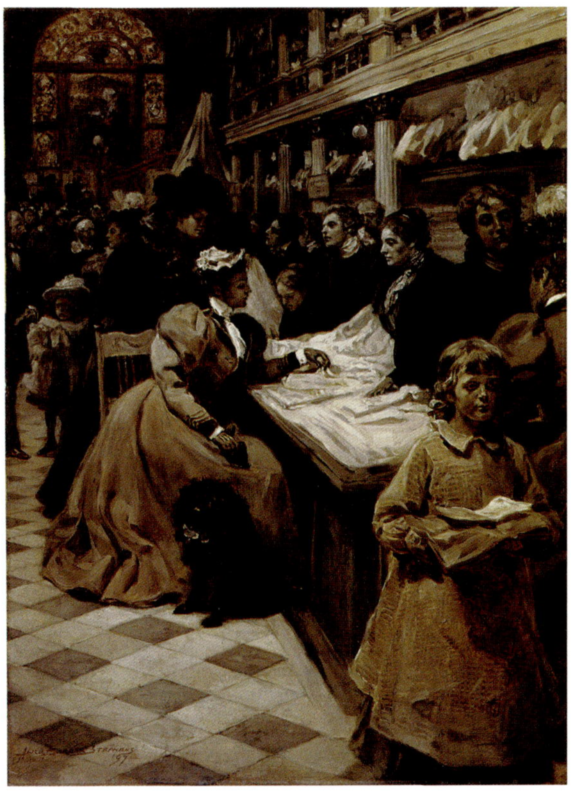

Figure 2
Alice Barber Stephens, *The Woman in Business, Ladies Home Journal,* September 1897, oil on canvas, 25 x 18 inches. Collection of the Brandywine River Museum, Chadds Ford, Pennsylvania. Museum Purchase, 1982. Acquisition made possible through Ray and Beverly Sacks.
IN EXHIBITION

William Sidney Mount's densely loaded *Fair Exchange, No Robbery* (1865), for instance, participates in a larger pattern of cultural critique through a set of codes that might otherwise be lost in a crowd of interesting genre paintings (fig. 1). The painting is a send-up of the Modern Times utopian community on the artist's native Long Island, an anarchist group that wanted to reform society by reconfiguring monetary exchange. Led by the indefatigable Josiah Warren, the movement circulated "equity notes" and "labor notes," representing work performed, in place of currency. Joining the notes was a barter system, although in both cases detractors wondered how to determine the worth of an individual's labor. Several contemporaries accused the Warrenites of the very usury and bloated capitalism for which they offered a panacea. Lampooning the group's motto of "Fair exchange, no robbery" (taken from Byron), Mount shows a tramp making a less-than-fair exchange of his threadbare hat for a mint-condition one atop a scarecrow. The conservative artist depicts a shabby farmer fenced off from the stalks of corn, which were also considered currency in Modern Times, and which, not coincidentally, appeared in Mount's drawings on banknotes.[3] Finally, Mount's painted critique reminds us that money itself was—and is—no static category, but rather an abstract concept that has been reconfigured on an as-needed basis.[4]

Another theme, discussed in the following pages but worthy of much lengthier examination, is that of women's roles in emergent market and corporate cultures. Alice Barber Stephens's painting *The Woman in Business,* commissioned for *Ladies' Home Journal* in 1897, gives us a sense of the

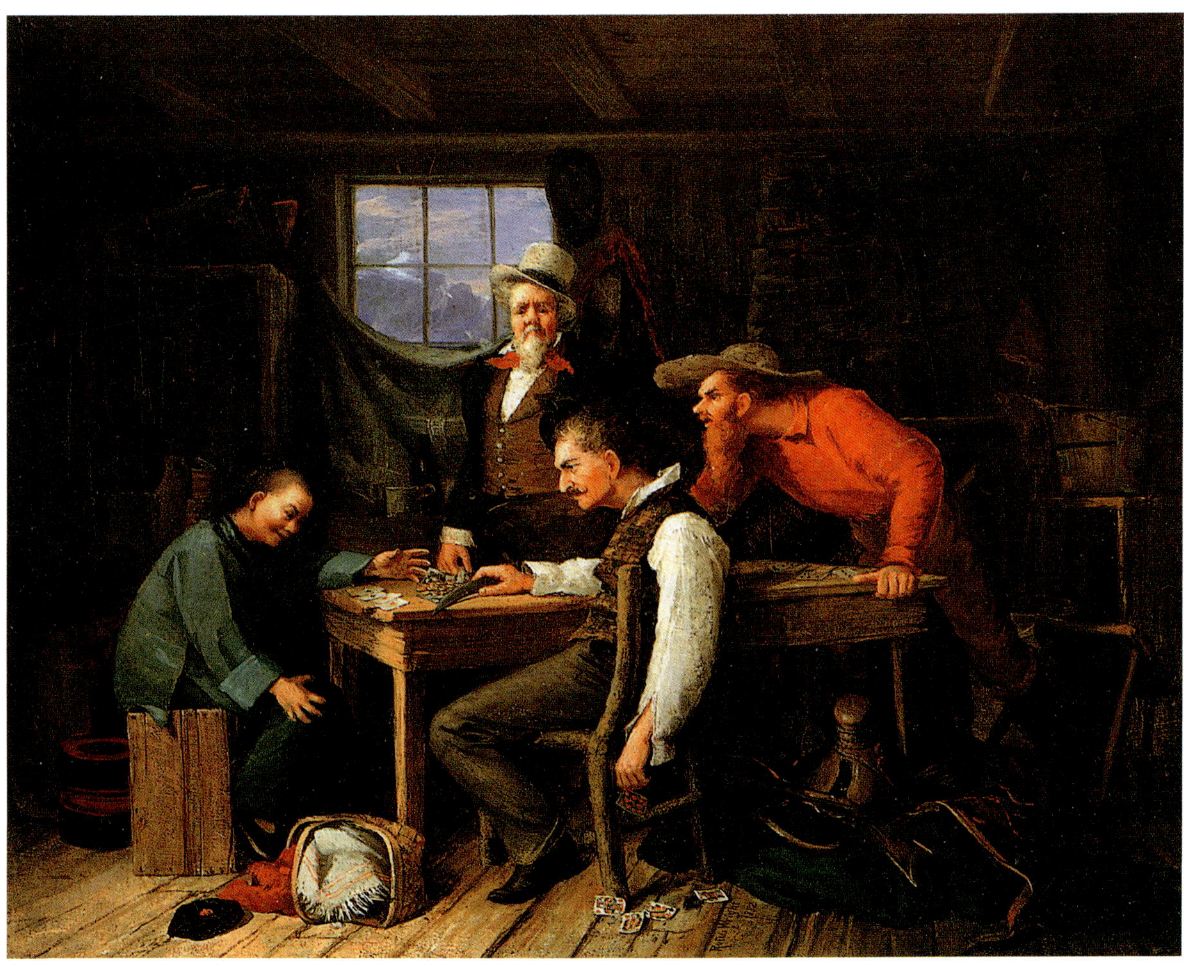

Figure 3
Rufus Wright, *The Card Players*, 1882, oil on canvas, 24½ x 29½ inches. Oakland Museum of Art, Kahn Collection.

complexity and consequences of gender, sexual difference, and financial ambition in late nineteenth-century America (fig. 2). The illustration bears witness to the increasing presence of women in clerical occupations: 5 percent in 1880; 18 percent in 1890; and 27 percent in 1900.[5] The image was one of six the *Journal* ordered from the artist for "The American Woman: A Series of Sketches." Depicting two sides of a sales counter at Wanamaker's department store in Philadelphia, Stephens represents not only the financially able and socially progressive "new woman" but also the socioeconomic infrastructure on which her putative autonomy depended.[6] Women, that is, were buyers and sellers—sometimes, as Stephens's illustration suggests, at the same time. Prescribing a sort of ongoing etiquette guide for proper womanhood, *Ladies' Home Journal* enlisted Stephens to do for the publication what the female clerk did for Wanamaker's: sell a narrowly circumscribed idea of femininity, one commensurate with women's immersion in the world of retail, and one that softened any sense of power suggested therein.[7] For women in service and clerical professions, as with their counterparts in middle-class homes, agency remained elusive.[8]

Administrative and service-oriented positions, as seen in Stephens's drawing, were held almost exclusively by native-born, Anglo, literate women. Immigrant women, as with immigrant men, were much more likely to be employed in strenuous and frequently tedious production and manufacturing jobs.[9] The pages that follow touch on taxing visions of race, but these, like the intersection of capitalism and nativism in general, merit further study. Works such as Charles M. Russell's *Not a Chinaman's Chance* (1893; Amon Carter Museum of Art) and Rufus Wright's *The Card Players* (1882) point to anti-Asian sentiment in the American west, portraying ethnic relations as a game in which the Other inevitably loses, or is at least—as in the Wright image—accused of cheating if he wins (fig. 3). A similar theme—life as a gamble in which money symbolizes something much greater at stake than playing cards—also characterizes Eanger Irving Couse's *The Card Player* (ca. 1897; location unconfirmed).[10] A presumably murdered Indian lies adjacent to a smoldering fire, cards strewn about the foreground. This image points to the tragic nexus of value, land, and American Indian policy, another subject that deserves careful study. Russell's *Not a Chinaman's Chance* and John Rogers's *The Foundling* (1870) suggest as well that genre *sculpture* is as revealing a site of taxing visions as genre *painting* and other two-dimensional media (fig. 4).

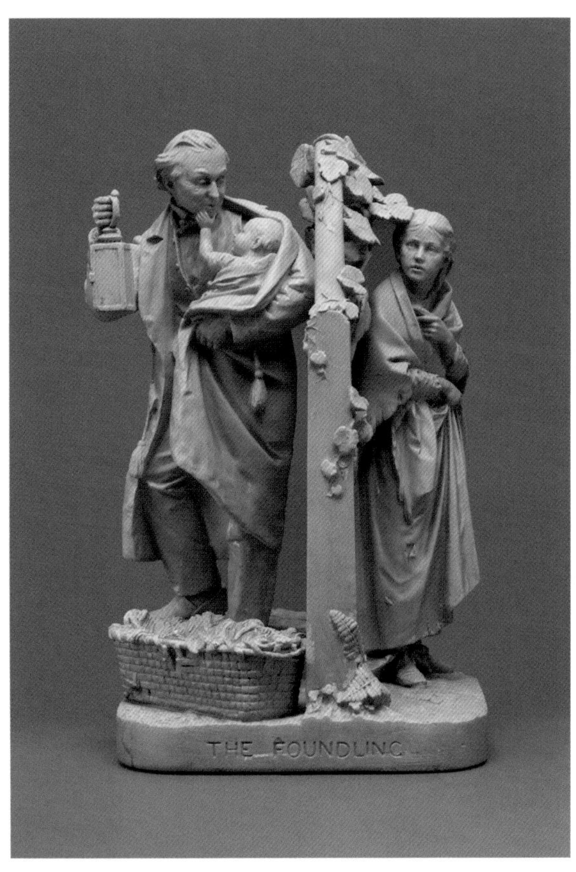

Figure 4
John Rogers, *The Foundling*, 1870, painted plaster, 21 inches (h). The Bronson Collection.

Agency, intention, and autonomy themselves, always tricky concepts in the history of art, become ever more complicated where monetary value and commercial exchange inform subject matter and otherwise intersect with artistic production. Of course, it is difficult to think of works of art that do not at some level meet the latter criteria. Yet the "taxing" genre foregrounds the question of just what methodologies best illuminate formal and thematic dynamics. In this project we have obviously gravitated toward formal and iconographical approaches, often in the service of issues of patronage, class, and labor. We understand, however, that this modest publication scrapes only the tip of the iceberg, and that several pictures benefit from other approaches, avenues of investigation that in many cases transcend the immediate scope—and budget, and availability of pictures—of the present project. For a critical introduction to the methodological possibilities of taxing pictures, we direct readers to Meredith Davis's 2006 dissertation, "Fool's Gold: American Trompe L'oeil Painting in the Golded Age," among other sources. In her discussion, for example, of Ferdinand Danton's painting

Figure 5
Ferdinand Danton, *Time is Money*, 1894, oil on canvas, 16 15/16 x 21 1/8 inches. Wadsworth Atheneum Museum of Art, Hartford, Connecticut. The Ella Gallup Sumner and Mary Catlin Sumner Fund, 1943.93. Photo: Wadsworth Atheneum Museum of Art/Art Resource, New York.

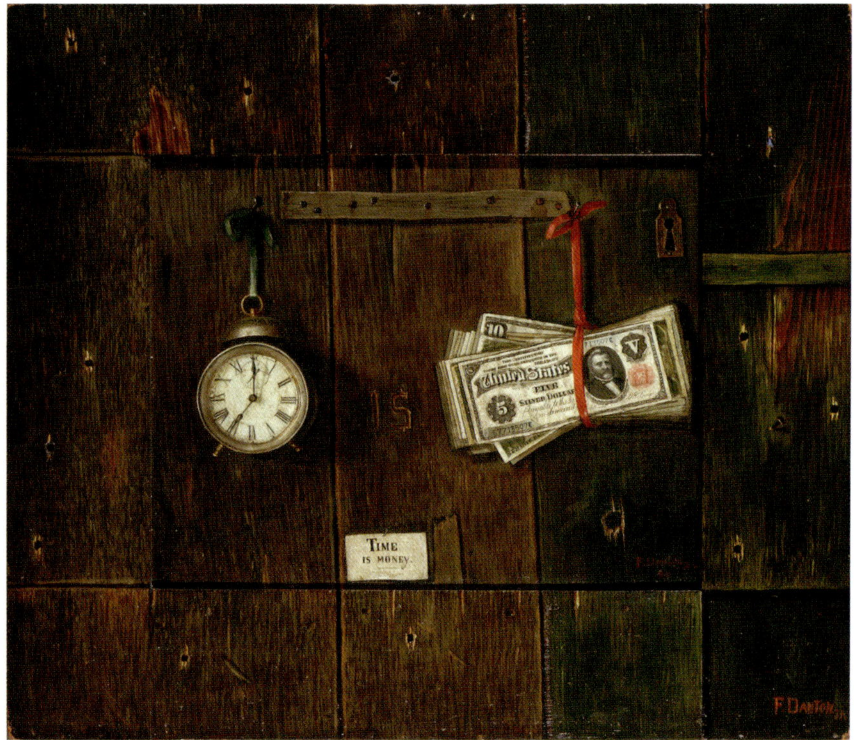

Time is Money (1894) and related pictures, Davis shows that our understanding benefits from going beyond the source of the title (Benjamin Franklin's *Advice to a Young Tradesman* [1748]), and even beyond the perhaps obvious connections to working environments increasingly enlisting the scientific management systems of Frederick Winslow Taylor and other Progressive era reformers (fig. 5). She encourages us to temper these considerations with other meditations on the time-is-money equation, a trajectory that extends from Karl Marx to Georg Simmel to Jacques Derrida.[11] We have obviously benefitted from these and other takes on the subject, and we hope this exhibition and catalogue join Davis's and related studies in stimulating a re-thinking not only of subject matter but also of approach.

We do, however, include several vexing pictures attesting to the evolving iconography of class bifurcation within the ripe (and admittedly complex) contexts of post–Civil War and Gilded Age America. We have aimed to unpack these complicated works, often to find yet more "baggage." In this, our ideas are indebted to the groundbreaking work on American genre painting by Patricia Hills and Elizabeth Johns, as well as the most recent museum exhibition devoted to the subject, the Metropolitan Museum of Art's *American Stories*, organized by Barbara Weinberg and Carrie Rebora Barratt in 2009.[12] Because of the comprehensiveness of previous scholarship, we have focused on a narrower selection of objects, many of which highlight the social and economic rigidity and even hopelessness that arose in tandem with increasing industrialization and urbanization. Other works register responses to the period's major financial panics and monetary crises, from the Civil War through the early Progressive era. It is our hope that *Taxing Visions* gives rise to other, perhaps even more focused, forays into financially engaged subject matter and the interpretive strategies they demand.

1. On the history of economic turmoil in the late nineteenth century, see Samuel Rezneck, *Business Depressions and Financial Panics: Essays in American Business and Economic History* (New York: Greenwood, [1968]). Systemic, technological, and organizational changes to American business are discussed in Alfred D. Chandler Jr., *The Visible Hand: The Managerial Revolution in American Business* (Cambridge, Mass.: Belknap Press of Harvard University Press, 1977); the social and cultural implications of these changes are addressed by Alan Trachtenberg in *The Incorporation of America: Culture and Society in the Gilded Age* (New York: Hill and Wang, 1982).

2. See Linda Henefield Skalet, "The Market for American Painting in New York, 1870–1915" (PhD diss., John Hopkins University, 1980); and Kevin M. Murphy, "Economics of Style: The Business Practices of American Artists and the Structure of the Market, 1850–1910" (PhD diss., University of California at Santa Barbara, 2005).

3. Our understanding of the painting is deeply indebted to Charles Colbert, "*Fair Exchange No Robbery*: William Sidney Mount's Commentary on Modern Times," *American Art* 8 (Summer–Autumn 1994): 29–41.

4. See Viviana A. Zelizer, *The Social Meaning of Money: Pin Money, Paychecks, Poor Relief, and Other Currencies* (New York: Basic Books, 1994).

5. William L. Barney, *The Passage of the Republic: An Interdisciplinary History of Nineteenth-Century America* (Lexington, Mass.: D. C. Heath, 1987), 328.

6. The site is identified as Wanamaker's in Eleanor Tufts, *American Women Artists, 1830–1930* (Washington, D.C.: International Exhibitions Foundation for the National Museum of Women in the Arts, 1987), 112, no. 44.

7. Renée Simon Klorman, "Selling Womanhood Back to Women: Alice Barber Stephens's 'American Woman Series,' 1897" (M.A. thesis, Sarah Lawrence College, 2002), 3, 6, 9. In the same issue graced by *The Woman in Business* on its cover, the magazine's male editor wrote a column that praised women who stayed in the household and thus steered clear of materialism and decadence, the impending "sewer of their minds" to which the workaday world leads; ibid., 16.

8. Zelizer, *The Social Meaning of Money*, 36–70.

9. Barney, *Passage of the Republic*, 328.

10. Couse's *The Card Player* is illustrated in William H. Gerdts, *Art Across America: Two Centuries of Regional Painting in America*, 3 vols. (New York: Abbeville Press, 1990), 3:193.

11. Meredith Paige Davis, "Fool's Gold: American Trompe L'oeil Painting in the Golded Age" (PhD diss., Columbia University, 2006), 208–10. Also exemplary is Jennifer Ann Greenhill, "The Plague of Jocularity: Contesting Humor in American Art and Culture, 1863–1893" (PhD diss., Yale University, 2007). Taylor's ideas are expounded in *The Principles of Scientific Management* (New York: Harper & Brothers, 1911).

12. Patricia Hills, *The Painters' America: Rural and Urban Life, 1810–1910* (New York: Praeger, [1974]); Elizabeth Johns, *American Genre Painting: The Politics of Everyday Life* (New Haven: Yale University Press, 1991); H. Barbara Weinberg and Carrie Rebora Barratt, eds. *American Stories: Paintings of Everyday Life, 1765–1915* (New York: Metropolitan Museum of Art, 2009).

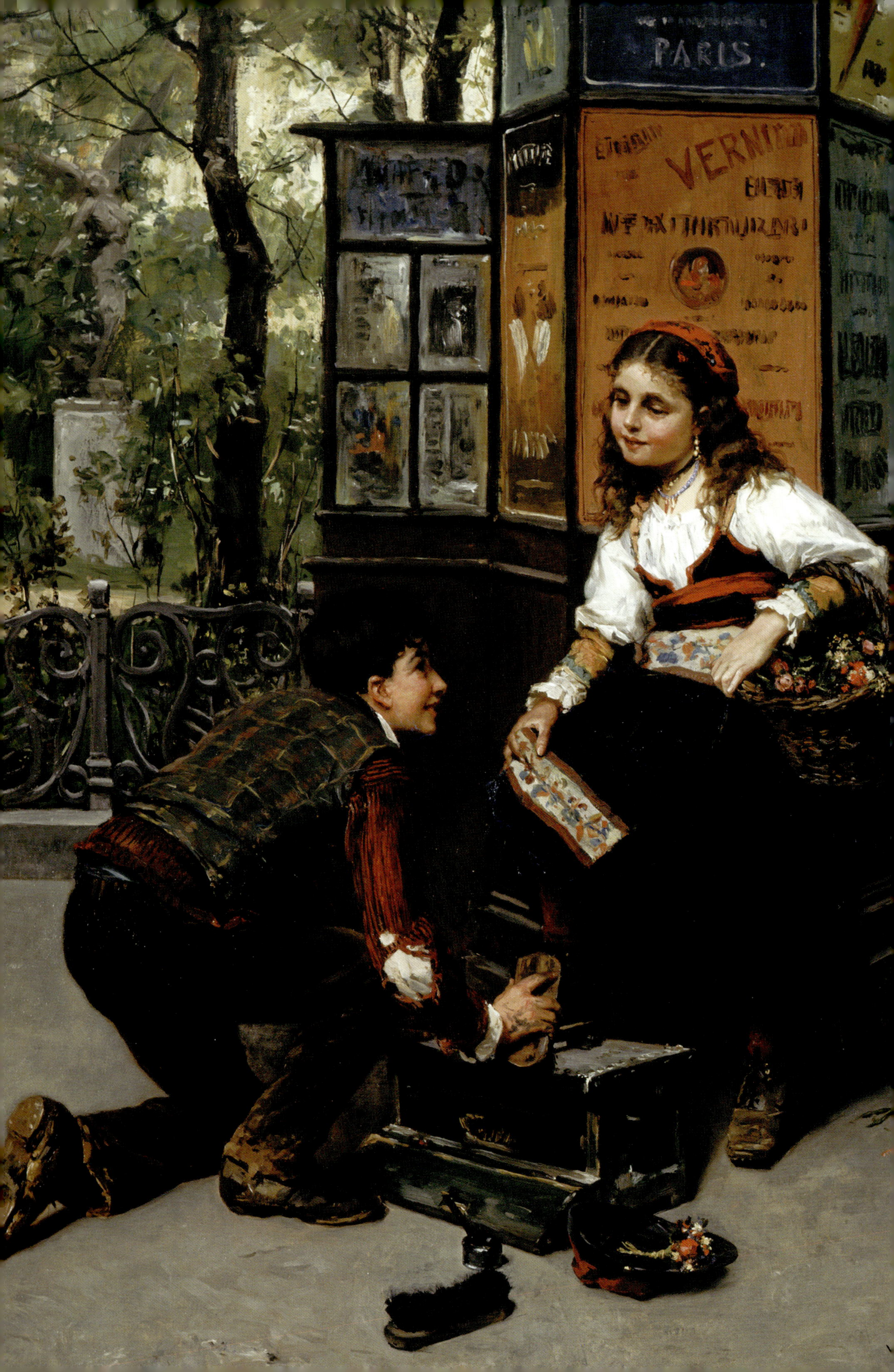
PARIS.

Taxing Visions and the "Decent Distance"

LEO G. MAZOW

At the beginning of the twenty-first century, a number of mobile home parks fronted North Atherton Street, a heavily traveled thoroughfare in State College, Pennsylvania, adjacent to University Park, home of The Pennsylvania State University. Several of them were within walking distance of a Wal-Mart, where many of the park inhabitants may have worked or shopped. These micro-communities within, and yet at the fringe of, State College visually ruptured the fabric of middle-class and upscale retail outlets, a fissure that blocked well-landscaped turnoffs into more affluent neighborhoods. As the years went by, several of the parks disappeared from sight—or at least from viewing distance of Atherton Street. With startling speed and efficiency, landowners and contractors emptied the lots and laid foundations for high-end coffee shops, car washes, banks, and cellular telephone outlets. Some of the mobile living spaces appear to have been pushed back from Atherton; some have merged to make way for stores; others are simply gone. It is as though the parks and their tenants have been pushed aside, concealed, or just dissolved in the name of progress. Pedestrians and commuters are now less burdened by the sight of those less fortunate individuals consigned to what one local real estate developer referred to as a "decaying asset."[1]

In parts of the United States, the presence of a mobile home demonstrably lessens the value of nearby permanent residences.[2] Some social phenomena, some images, indeed try—or tax—our sensibilities more than others, leading to decisions by land developers and other entrepreneurs to alter the lay of the land, and thus change the flow of business, living, and socializing. There is nothing new—or necessarily American—about this phenomenon; few things are more ubiquitous than the sight of poverty and the concomitant strategies to avoid seeing it and render it less visible or at least more palatable. In art, the subject of poverty has taken on compelling form over the past few centuries, and especially so in the second half of the nineteenth century, from the Panic of 1857 through about 1900. During the Civil War, Reconstruction, and Gilded Age, immigration, industrialization, and urbanization altered forever the look, tempo, and experience of daily life. It is little wonder that visual artists time and again registered these momentous

Opposite
Detail of figure 9.

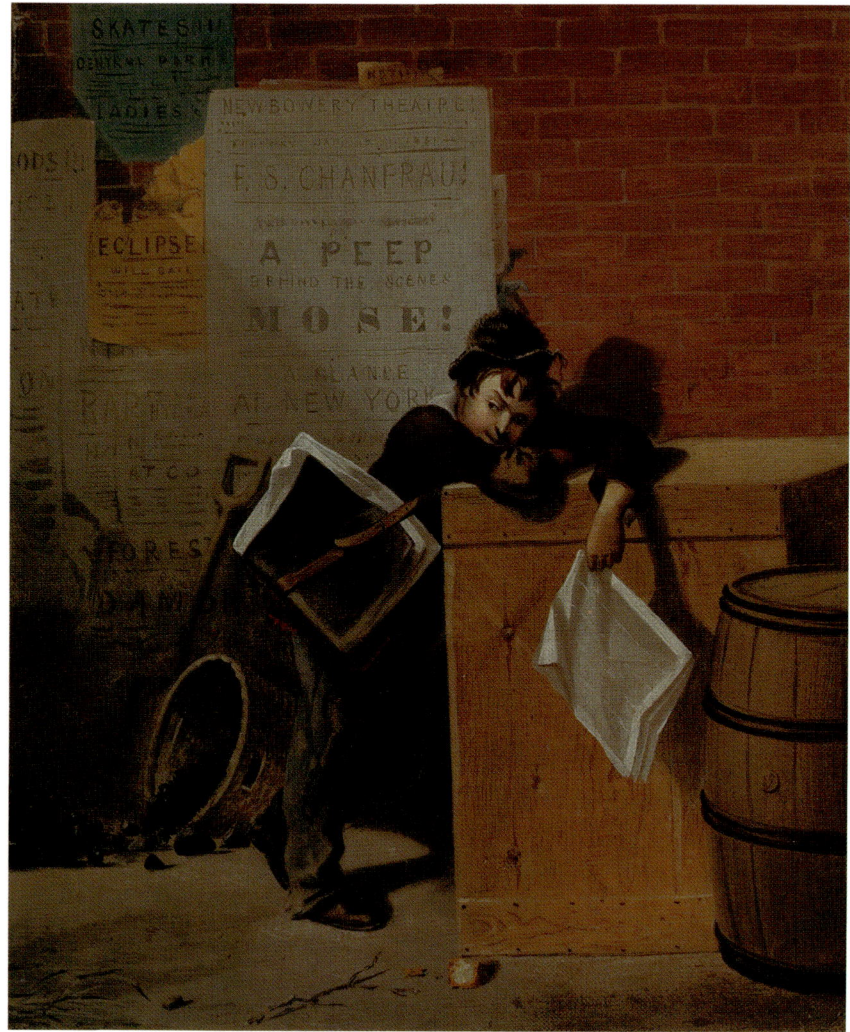

Figure 6
James Henry Cafferty, *The Weary Newsboy*, 1861, oil on canvas, 12 3/8 x 9 7/8 inches. Palmer Museum of Art, The Pennsylvania State University. Purchased with funds from the Terra Art Enrichment. Fund, 2003.23.
IN EXHIBITION

changes—macro and micro alike—in their works. And yet, with only a few important exceptions, the American art historical canon elides this subgenre of artistic production.[3] Like so many less-than-picturesque trailer parks on Atherton, it taxes our sensibilities.

As for the recurring iconography of poverty-borne despair in nineteenth-century American painting and sculpture, the twentieth- and early twenty-first-century art market itself can be seen as enacting a certain shoving aside first prophesied in the works of art themselves. Predictably, and with only occasional, if notable, exceptions, any prolonged survey of auction catalogues demonstrates the enormous price differential between leisure-laden Impressionist and Tonalist landscapes and depictions of labor and hardship in those painted fields. Sentimental, uplifting, and psychologically intriguing landscapes, class-conscious portraits, and fancy genre pieces are invariably reproduced larger and closer to the front of a catalogue than are pictures of the mind-numbing activity of businessmen and hirelings, the struggles of workers, or the tedious process of running a business. Some patrons may just not want to meditate upon the imagery of a day laborer realizing his job was lost to the sluggish economy. Who wants to see the awkward meeting of capital and labor when no shortage of leisurely landscapes and portraits allows us to put our minds elsewhere? But the larger trend merits underscoring: pictures of taxing visions are often sidestepped, banished, overlooked, and otherwise treated in a manner comparable to the downtrodden subjects that appear within them.

Shoving aside that which taxes us is precisely the social problem tackled by nineteenth-century American artists who depicted the alternately sentimental and vexing subject of newsboys. Like other children working on the streets during this period, newsboys served as precious fodder for reform crusades and sentimental literature, and yet they were condemned, one historian observes, as "street rats and guttersnipes, vagrants and beggars."[4] James Henry Cafferty's *The Weary Newsboy* (1861) portrays an urban alcove in which a less-than-successful peddler sulks (fig. 6).[5] An unused shovel and spilt coals join the unsold newspapers as signs of work unfinished and promise unfulfilled—like the half-eaten bread below, "fruits" the newsboy has yet to taste. On the brick wall directly behind the peddler, a bill advertises a production featuring the ever-popular urban folk hero who stood against—and wreaked havoc on—injustice: Mose the Bowery Boy. The poster promotes several Mose productions, including *A Glance at New York*, with Frank Chanfrau starring as Mose, at the New Bowery Theatre on January 26–27, 1861.[6] Equal parts fireman, jokester, rowdy, dandy, moralizing hero, and trash-talking brawler, Mose was, as one chronicler put it, "buffoon, champion, and guardian angel of the Bowery."[7] Mose could hand-deliver horsecars from one part of town to another, yet Cafferty's figure can barely hold his papers.[8] The irony is that the weary newsboy represents precisely the browbeaten child championed by the giant folk hero.

Two diminutive newsboys also occupy the foreground of Cafferty's collaborative painting with Charles G. Rosenberg, *Wall Street, Half Past Two O'Clock*, October 13, 1857 (1858), suggesting that this cute-if-squalid waif became momentarily important during a breakdown of rule and order (in this case the Panic of 1857) (fig. 38). The newsboy motif populates paintings by other antebellum and Civil War–era artists as well, but in the years following the war, John George Brown emerged as the most renowned and skillful appropriator of the child peddler image, with his hawkers of periodicals and flowers, shiners of shoes, and performers of street music. Works like Brown's *A Tough Story* (1886) exemplify the lengths to which artists and authors went to create and market a taste for child labor rendered picturesque, portraying children who, unlike Cafferty's newsboy, need not be "shoved aside" (fig. 7). In addition to cleansing and glossing over the daily toil of the Irish immigrant

Figure 7
John George Brown, *A Tough Story*, 1886, oil on canvas, 25 x 30 1/8 inches. North Carolina Museum of Art, Raleigh. Purchased with funds from the State of North Carolina.

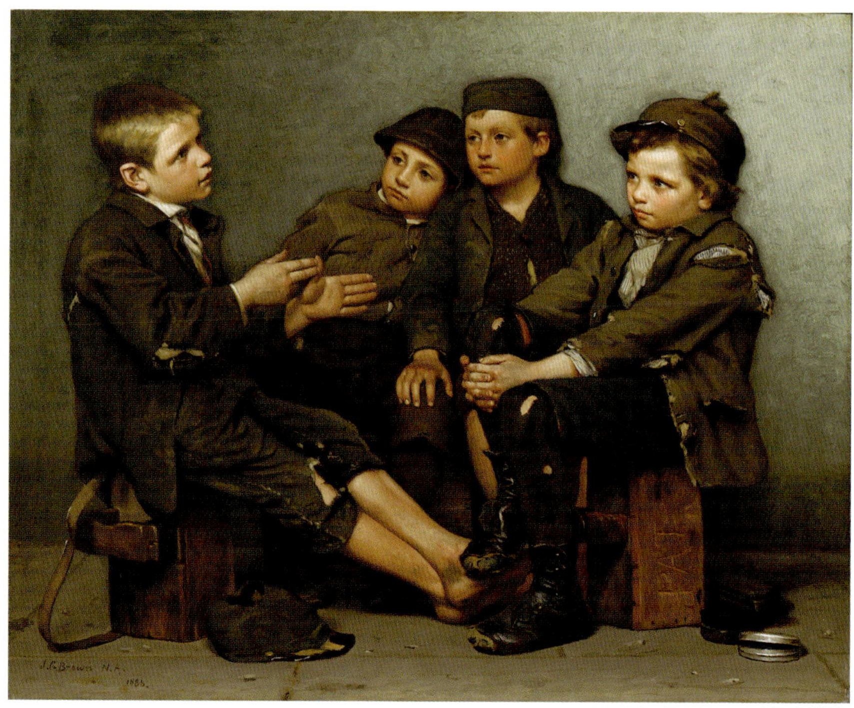

"ragamuffin," *A Tough Story* depicts the child raconteur, that increasingly familiar bootblack or news seller who, in addition to peddling wares, literally sold his or her story to interested passersby.[9] That spruced-up—or perhaps, in the context of the present exhibition, *un-taxed*—version of urban employment appealed to an emergent class of entrepreneurs, including William T. Evans, John Jacob Astor, Cornelius Vanderbilt, and Isidor Straus, the latter a department-store magnate who eventually owned Macy's, and who lent a number of his Brown paintings to the World's Columbian Exposition.[10] In 1886, when Brown was asked about his practice of limning "bootblacks" with "clean faces" in spite of their "dirty clothes," he responded, "If you paint them with dirty faces you can't sell the picture."[11] In these pictures Brown distanced the abject and foregrounded the cleansed and marketable, not unlike the supplanting of trailer parks by new commercial developments on North Atherton Street.

It would be a mistake, however, to classify Brown's entire artistic production as sanitized exigency. Adding to the complex task of interpreting Brown's and other artists' academically informed, seemingly disinfected imagery is a striking paradox: even middling reformers worried about and frequently actively campaigned against both private and public subsidized relief for the poor.[12] Brown's paintings surely appealed to patrons' fluctuating and sometimes fickle sentiments toward the indigent. Several pictures are indeed, perhaps necessarily, ambivalent—neither taxing nor reassuring, with robustness, cuteness, and coquettishness only partially offsetting the

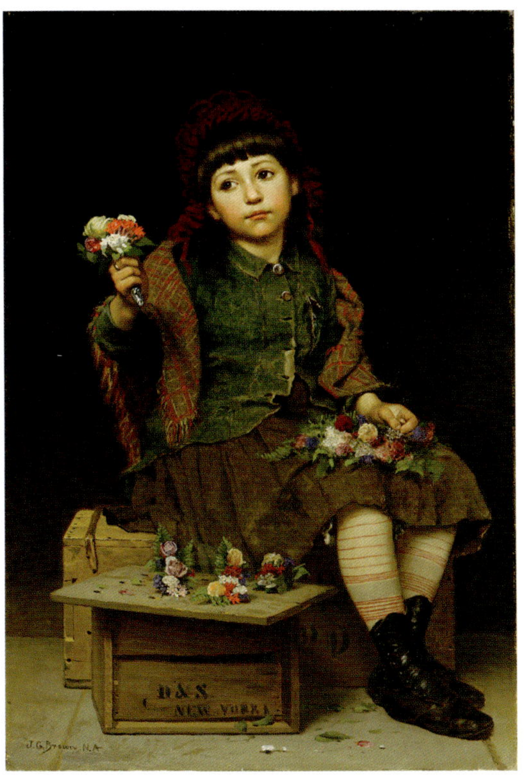

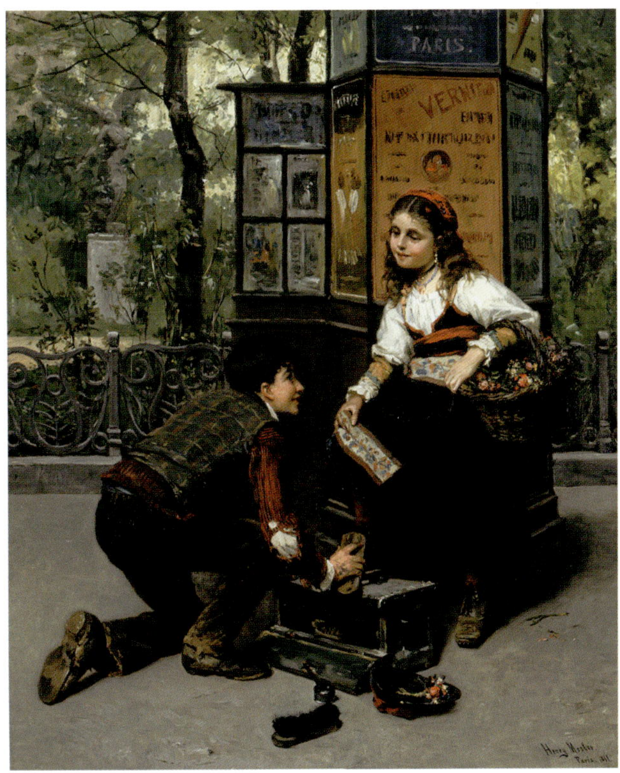

sense of impending physical danger or retail failure. Brown's *Buy a Posy* (ca. 1881) is one such work that does not fit neatly into an either-or interpretation (fig. 8). The subject's clothing and well-groomed hair recall the artist's trademark sentimentalizing, but her pouting countenance challenges recurring depictions of girls as agents of moral and marketing suasion. Repeating with the tilt of her head the leaning—if not yet wilting—of the flowers, the ruddy-cheeked girl is, nonetheless, not exactly passive. She is selling what for centuries has been an emblem of female purity, with Brown, intentionally or unwittingly, joining other artists in destabilizing increasingly anachronistic ideals equating the floral with feminine beauty and fecundity.[13] Historically, posies and nosegays were marketed as ornaments for women's bodies or clothing, and, in certain works of American and British literature, their presentation as gifts offered suitors a means of stating their affections.[14]

The posy similarly stands for mitigated sweetness in Henry Mosler's *The Fair Exchange* (1881; fig. 9). Dressed in a presumably Norwegian bunad, a girl offers a piece of her embroidered fabric to a bootblack, perhaps to accompany the posy that has fallen from her basket into his hat. The verso of the painting is inscribed, "painted to order for Knoedler," the transatlantic dealer in paintings and prints.[15] The picture illuminates Parisian street life while retaining the academic drawing and formal sumptuousness that were so very important to Knoedler & Company when the firm commissioned

Figure 8
John George Brown, *Buy a Posy*, ca. 1881, oil on canvas, 23⅞ x 15¼ inches. North Carolina Museum of Art. Given in memory of Mr. and Mrs. E. J. Ellisberg by their children.
IN EXHIBITION

Figure 9
Henry Mosler, *The Fair Exchange*, 1881, oil on canvas, 35 x 28 inches. Cincinnati Art Museum. Gift of The Procter & Gamble Company, 2003.88.
IN EXHIBITION

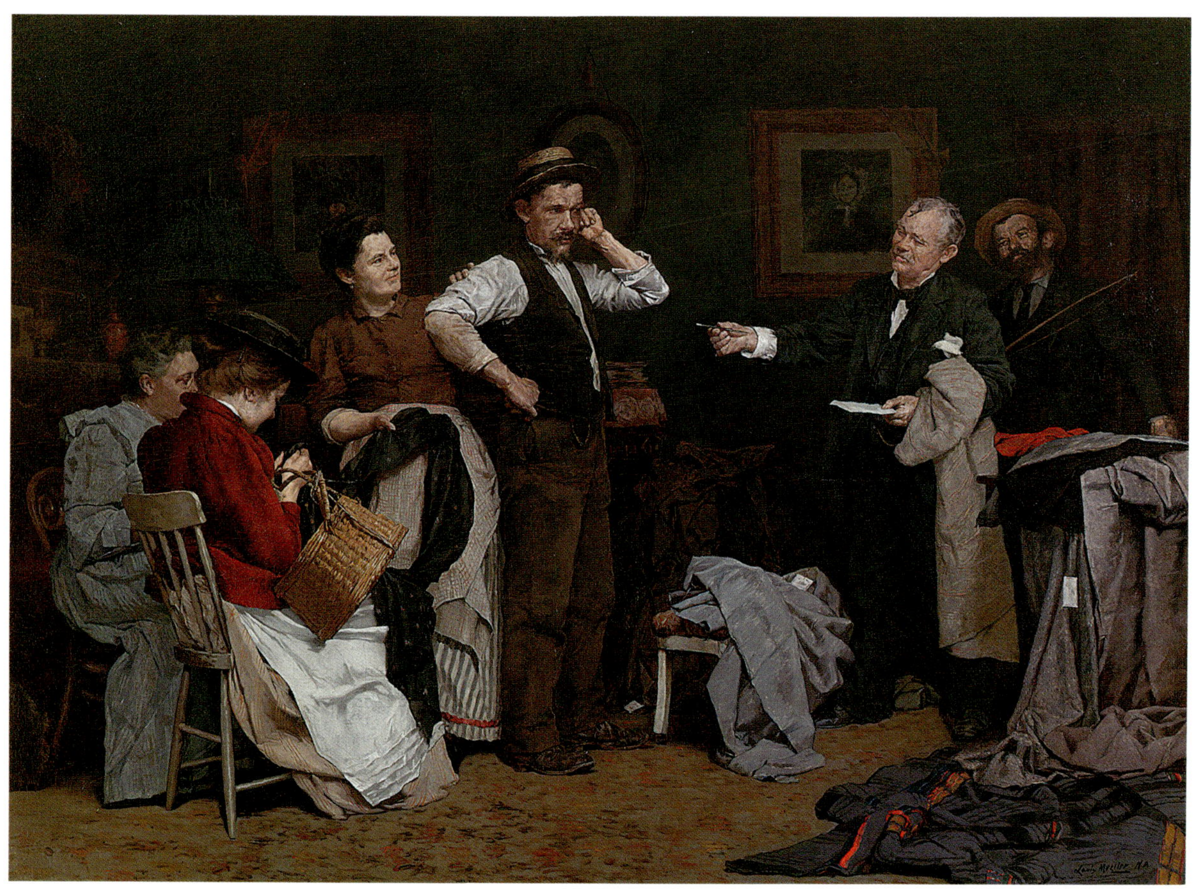

Figure 10
Louis Moeller, *Sign Here*, ca. 1890s, oil on canvas, 30 x 40 inches. Collection of Spanierman Gallery, LLC. Photo courtesy of Spanierman Gallery, LLC.
IN EXHIBITION

the image, presumably to circulate as a print. A Cincinnati-born artist working in Paris, Mosler seemed to understand, along with Brown, that a picture could only be so exotic or squalid—otherwise it would not sell. The bunad and the embroidered textile in the girl's hand—emblems of peasantry and ethnic difference—are integrated within the composition's cascade of forms, and the viewer's sensibilities are thereby all the less taxed.[16]

Several late nineteenth-century American artists used academically informed linear styles to produce slick, polished surfaces depicting financial ruin. It seems ironic that verisimilitude could offset the threat of subject matter—as in the case of John George Brown and Thomas Waterman Wood (see figs. 7, 8, 29). The work of the Munich-trained painter Louis Moeller enriches but also complicates such an interpretation, in part because we know relatively little about the artist (although he was certainly renowned in his lifetime),[17] and in part because of the deceptive simplicity of his heavily applied masses of color delineating an aesthetic bordering on hyperrealism. The artist's oeuvre can be divided into two categories of subject matter: individuals telling jokes, discussing news, and trading stories; and individuals reaching into their pockets for money, disagreeing over bills, debating the

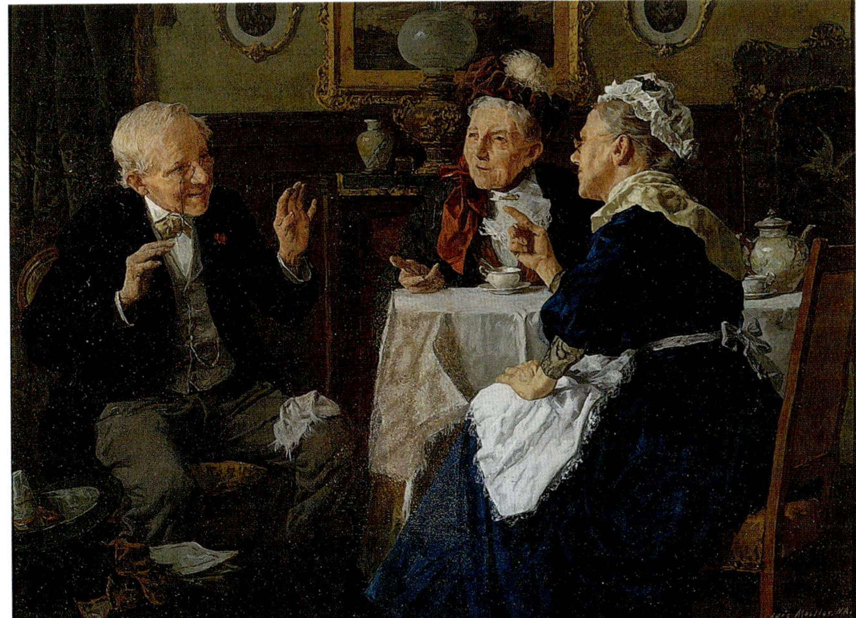

Figure 11
Louis Moeller, *The Will*, ca. 1896, oil on canvas, 18 x 24 inches. Garzoli Gallery, San Rafael, California.
IN EXHIBITION

value of objets d'art, receiving alms from passersby, settling financial matters, sadly selling off their belongings (fig. 10), and investing funds. Moeller's paintings frequently illustrate the climax of an argument, when civil niceties yield to impasse. The latter transpires in *The Will* (ca. 1896), where the tension of settling an estate interrupts an afternoon tea (fig. 11). The accusatory fingers of the women meet the defensive gesture of the man, who pulls out his chair as if to counter an assertion.

It is tempting to read a measure of personal experience into Moeller's heated financial conversations in paint. In order to make ends meet, Moeller was on occasion forced to abandon genre painting and work in decorative media.[18] As Kevin Murphy points out in his essay in this catalogue, his situation was (and obviously still is) not so unique. James Cafferty often needed to find additional "labor, which in many cases was barely profitable."[19] George Inness temporarily abandoned landscape painting and produced a series of pictures of veterans and other figural pieces in the early 1880s, expressly to "bring money readily, . . . command ready sale, and get out of debt" (see figs. 16, 17).[20] Surely something of this sentiment—the need for a quick financial fix—led Moeller into a lopsided business arrangement with the insatiable American collector Thomas B. Clarke. As the art historian William H. Gerdts has explained, "Moeller provided Clarke with paintings, including unframed studies and unfinished works, which Clarke could then commission the artist to complete."[21] Clarke's arrangement with Moeller was a modified version of the popular piecework plan, frequently instituted by employers in the 1870s and 1880s. Aiming to make laborers their own

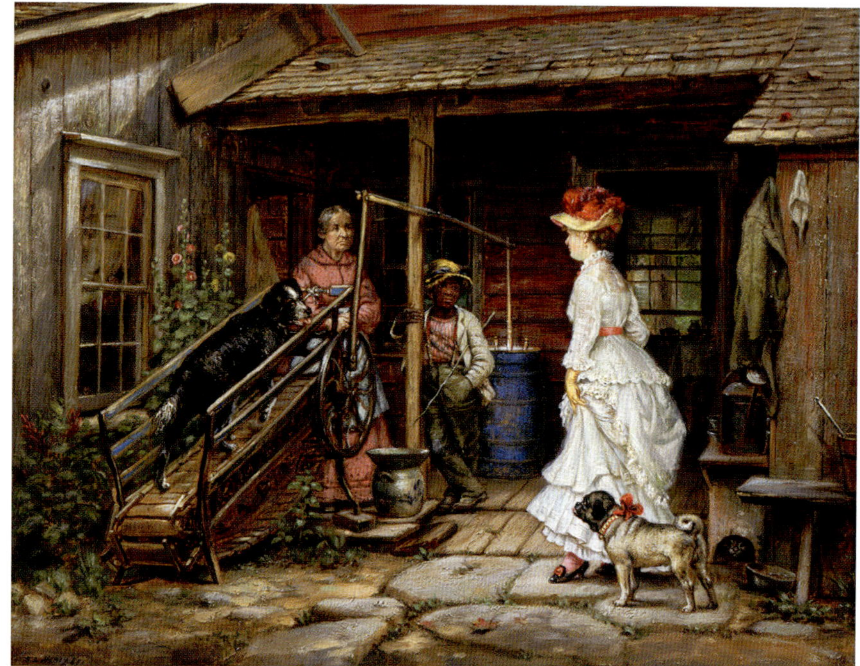

Figure 12
Edward Lamson Henry, *Capital and Labor*, 1881, oil on canvas, 12½ x 15⅜ inches. Courtesy of the New-York Historical Society, Gift of George A. Zabriskie, 1940.5.
IN EXHIBITION

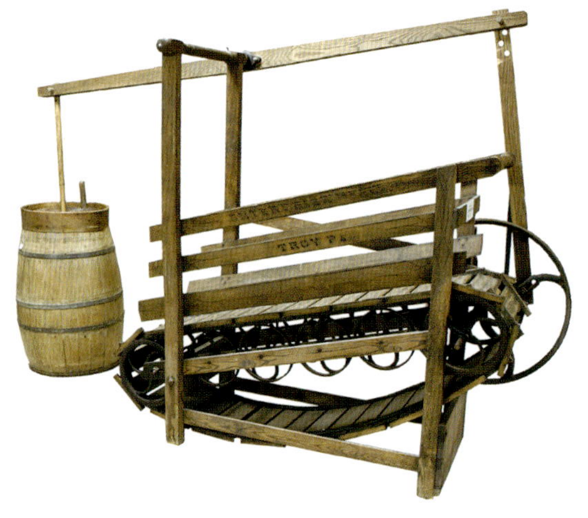

Figure 13
Dog-Powered Butter Churn, patented by H. M. Childs, Utica, New York, 1871, 1881. Pasto Agricultural Museum, The Pennsylvania State University. Photo: Greg Kordas.

bosses and permitting them to work at their own pace, the piecework movement offered hirelings the illusion of occupational emancipation at the price of regimentation and increased control over their production.[22] Further research on Moeller might link these cultural movements, the artist's financial circumstances, and his style and subject matter. This is not a call for biographical determinism—as if Moeller's paintings were simple reflections of his difficult straits—but rather a recognition that his paintings are more sophisticated than they may appear at first glance; that Moeller himself was effectively asked to "sign here" (see fig. 10); and that a picture of a disputed will or other legal document might resonate with the artist's own "will."[23]

In a yet more problematic manner, Edward Lamson Henry's painting *Capital and Labor* (1881) suggests the awkward intersections of haves and have-nots (fig. 12). In keeping with Henry's strategy of partitioning scenes into opposing zones, a well-dressed woman in white appears at right as a visitor, if an alien one, to a dilapidated servants' quarters, marked by peeling paint and decaying shingles and laterally framed by instruments of manual labor and house upkeep.[24] Perhaps most distressing is the black dog powering a butter-churning apparatus (to which the animal's neck is roped, like a noose); it seems the squalid antitype of the perky white pug at right. A contemporary notice of the painting found the pug "aristocratic." The red bow indeed links the animal to the right-hand zone of leisure and "capital" (the bow matches the woman's hat decorations).[25] Meant to relieve the burden of domestic labor and thereby preserve women's health, the dog-powered churn was patented in New York State in 1871, with an additional patent for improvements awarded in 1881 (fig. 13). *Capital and Labor* takes some artistic license with the steep angle of the churning mechanism, and it is likely that the dog would have fallen at such a slope—a sign perhaps intended, of "capital's" disregard for the sacrifices of "labor."[26]

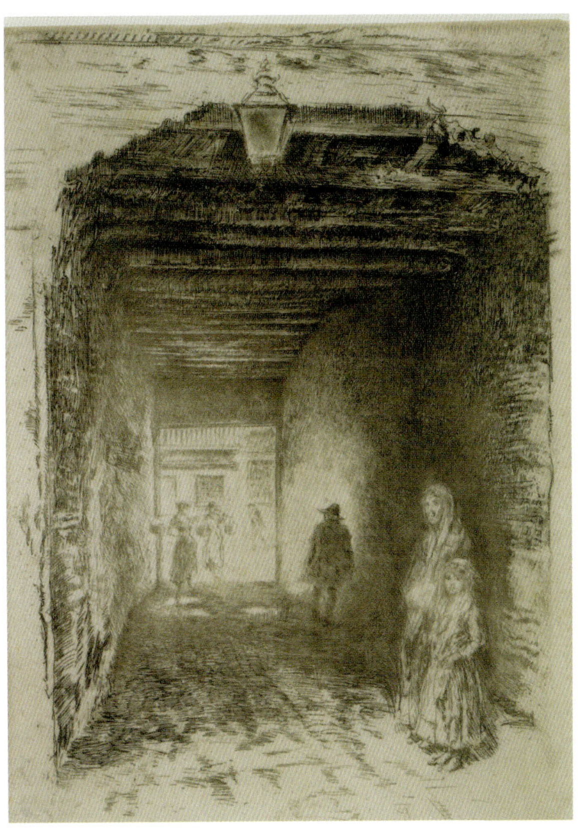

Figure 14
James McNeill Whistler, *Beggars*, ca. 1892, etching with drypoint on off-white paper, 11 15/16 x 8 5/16 inches. Terra Foundation for American Art, Chicago. Daniel J. Terra Collection, 1994.8. Photo: Terra Foundation for American Art, Chicago/Art Resource, NY.
IN EXHIBITION

Another contemporary notice of the Henry painting commented on the "poor old shepherd dog [at left], wearily walking a treadmill which grinds a churn."[27] By the 1880s, the word "dog" signified extreme overwork, often with no end in sight (as in the phrase "working like a dog"), and by the 1890s, the term "churning day" connoted the time reserved for a housewife's chores.[28] Such readily understood colloquialisms both enhance and intensify our reading of *Capital and Labor*. In spite of the signs of human labor and drudgery, it is ultimately the animal that carries the burden (in this logic, the elderly woman and African American child are treated as so many domesticated animals). In the final analysis, it may be possible to interpret *Capital and Labor* somewhat autobiographically. The piece could relate to Henry's well-known financial hardships or his repulsion at, and desire to distance himself from, the perceived lower rungs of class and ethnicity. In 1880, the artist described European immigrants as so much "sewage" and commented on "the encroachments of the low orders and their offspring here in New York." In this interpretation, we might view the meeting of "capital" and "labor," of haves and have-nots, just as the conservative artist's clientele may have seen it—awkward and unnatural.[29]

Distance and buffering from the impoverished Other are given compositional force in James McNeill Whistler's etching *Beggars* (ca. 1892 [first printed 1879–80]; fig. 14). Whereas Henry bisected the tableau laterally into realms of moneyed and indigent, the expatriate has envisioned a severely foreshortened Venice passageway with two female beggars seen from the vantage point of a passerby. As with Henry's *Capital and Labor*, Whistler's print resonates with his autobiography. In the wake of alienating his patron Frederick Leyland in

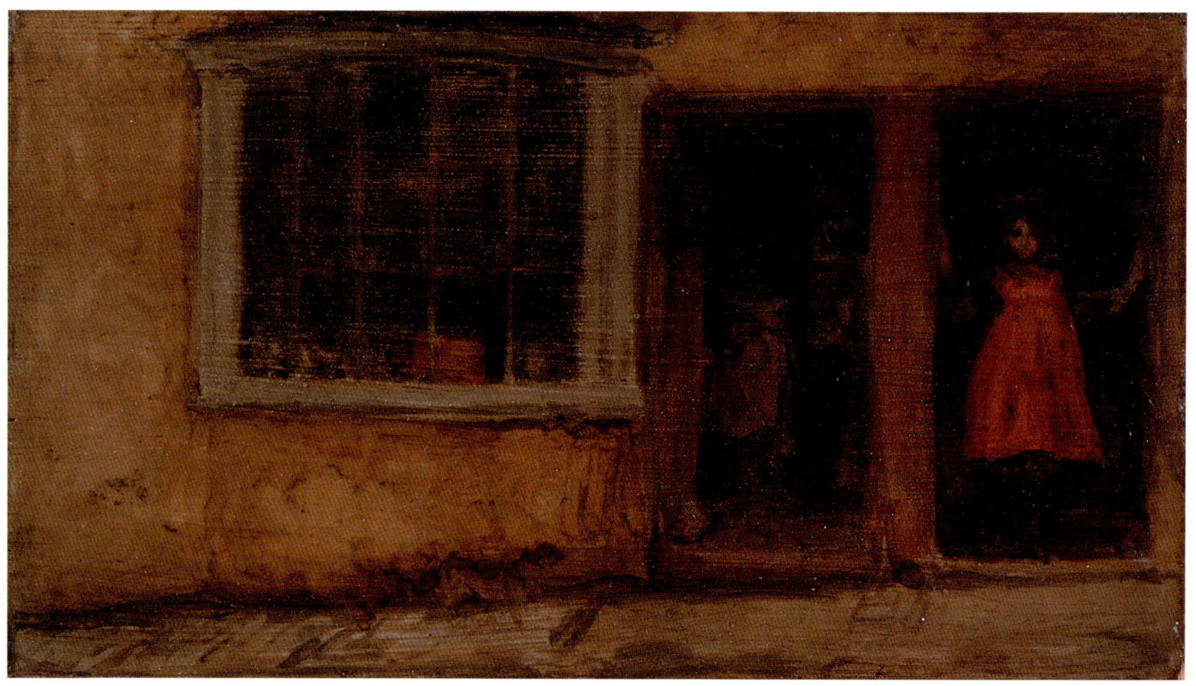

Figure 15
James McNeill Whistler, *Rose and Red: The Barber's Shop, Lyme Regis*, 1895, oil on wood panel, 4 7/8 x 8 1/4 inches. Georgia Museum of Art, University of Georgia. Eva Underhill Holbrook Memorial Collection of American Art, Gift of Alfred H. Holbrook, GMOA 1945.96.
IN EXHIBITION

1876 and suing John Ruskin for libel in late 1878—a suit the artist won, though he was awarded only a farthing—Whistler filed for bankruptcy. He saw in his Venetian etchings an opportunity to regain finances and critical favor.[30] Although not reduced to begging, he could afford only the most modest lodgings in Venice. He felt very self-conscious about his less-than-elegant lifestyle and, once there, was forced to request funds from Marcus Huish of the Fine Art Society in London, which had invested in the Venetian jaunt as a money-making enterprise.[31] Whistler scholar Alastair Grieve has observed that mendicants in fact would not have loitered in the private covered pathway, or *sottoportico*, between the Campo Santa Margarita and the Corte de le Carozze, pictured in Whistler's etching. The figures are included to appeal to the print's potential clientele in London, and to offer, one might suppose, some picturesque distance from the socioeconomic realm they inhabit.[32]

It can be difficult reconciling the oft-mentioned parallels between Whistler's precarious financial straits—his own understanding of begging—and the separation of high art and daily life that lay at the heart of the Aesthetic Movement and the related art-for-art's-sake philosophy, both of which Whistler championed. In 1881, an English critic commented of Whistler, "In the character of humanity he has not time to be interested," suggesting that the purpose of art was the attainment of rarefied ideals of beauty, not the delineation of narrative and subject matter.[33] Such a disconnect, in which human beings are reduced to compositional devices, renders both the subject matter and the modes of viewing in works like *Beggars* and *A Chelsea Shop*

(1894–95) all the more taxing (see fig. 36). By the time Whistler painted the latter, his early interest in documentary realism had all but disappeared. Any emphasis on working-class Chelsea or the iconography of want, of children peering through a window at goods, is offset and neutralized by the scene's reassuring and cleansing distance from artist and audience alike, as it is in any number of the artist's Chelsea subjects.[34] Whistler enlisted a similar distancing formula in his slightly later portrayals of Lyme Regis, a coastal town in Dorset, at the border with Devon. In *Rose and Red: The Barber's Shop, Lyme Regis* (1895), the artist depicts the seamier side to life in this otherwise middling seaside resort (fig. 15). As agricultural depression escalated in Dorset in the 1890s, the poor of Lyme Regis were relegated to employment in retail outlets and as domestic "help."[35] But in *The Barber's Shop*, the abstract shapes and moody coloring with which the shop and its denizens are depicted beckon our attention almost as much as the actual girl at right, the shadowy figures at left, and the large window. As if removing contemporary social history from the equation, lower class labor is here but a series of innocuous "notes," as the artist and his critics called them, in rose and red.

Art historian David Park Curry has commented on the contradictions between Whistler's gritty realism and Aestheticism's buffering distance; scholars have also noted Whistler's profound influences on, and his remarkable affinities with, his fellow American artists.[36] Particularly noteworthy is the case of landscape painter George Inness, who increasingly challenged the notion of painting as a merely formal exercise, as opposed to a socially and spiritually engaged vehicle. Like so many Americans of his generation, Inness was an activist on behalf of reformer-economist-journalist Henry George's Single Tax movement, which advocated for a tax based only on the land's promise for profit, and which called for a gradual shifting of all property from the hands of owner-capitalists to those of laborers. At a celebratory dinner alongside several fellow Single Taxers (including Henry George himself) in early 1890, Inness commented, "That which [one] does not create belongs to the community, and that is land." Intimately familiar with George's renowned tome *Progress and Poverty*, and taking seriously George's idea that manufactured products belonged to those who had manufactured them, Inness frequently claimed his right to pictures he had previously sold, attempting to retain the work or, more often, altering them as his thinking on the paintings evolved.[37]

An incident concerning Inness's *An Old Veteran* (ca. 1881) suggests the extent of his George-inspired producerism (fig. 16). When the owner of an Inness landscape found *Old Veteran* underneath another painting she had purchased, she claimed that Inness had sold her two paintings. Inness threatened to sue, commenting, "I suppose that if you bought a pair of shoes and found that a five-dollar bill had accidentally dropped into one of the shoes

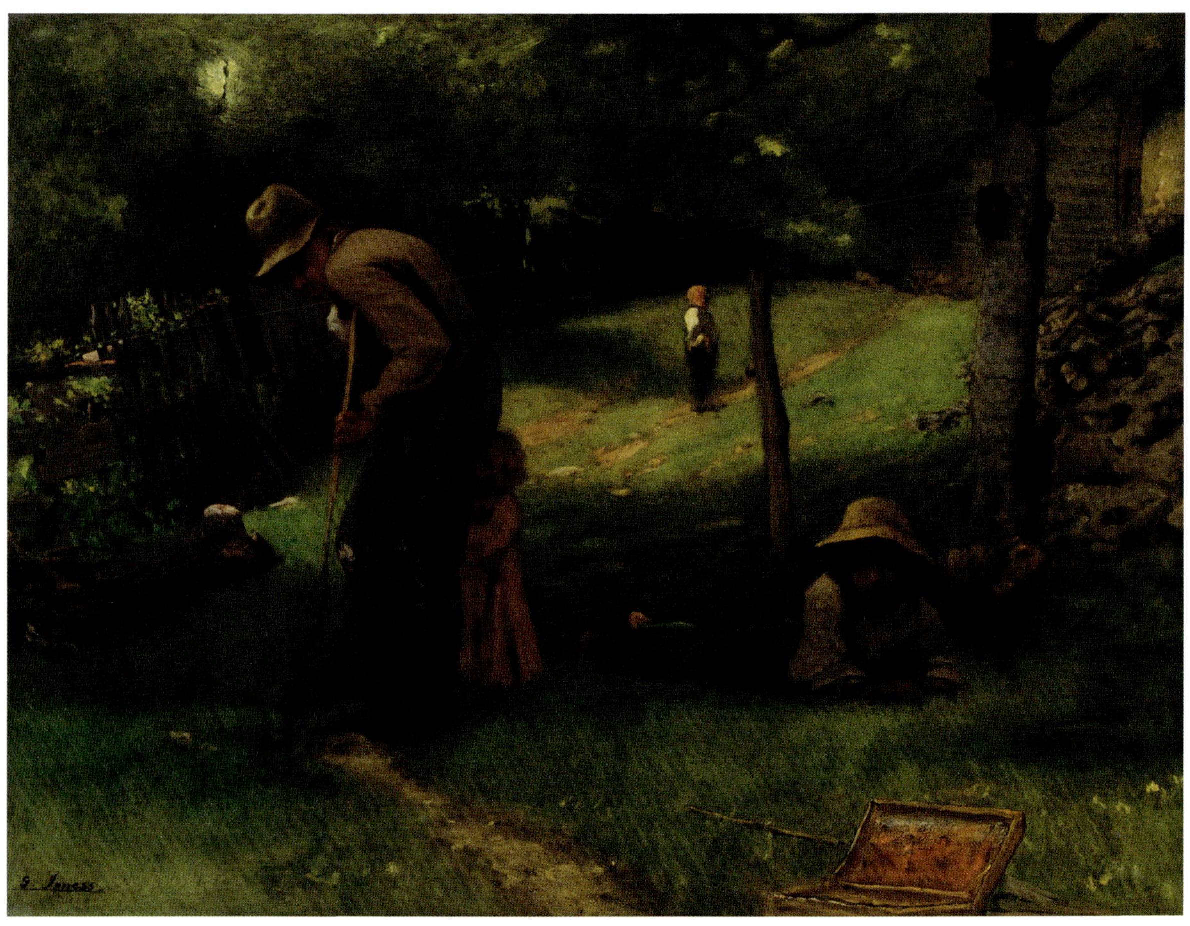

Figure 16
George Inness, *An Old Veteran*, ca. 1881, oil on canvas, 35 3/8 x 45 3/8 inches. Chrysler Museum of Art, Norfolk, Virginia. Gift of Walter P. Chrysler Jr., 71.662.

when the clerk was wrapping them up, you would keep the five dollars."[38] Artists, illustrators, and writers in George's Single Tax movement called for an honest, unsentimental, nothing-held-back realism in their respective media, and the renewed emphasis on figure painting in Inness's work in the early 1880s owes much to this approach.[39]

Another work from Inness's veteran series, alternately called *In the Gloaming* or *The Old Veteran* (ca. 1881–83; fig. 17), foregoes the heroism, moralizing, and sublimity of Winslow Homer's *The Veteran in a New Field* (1865; Metropolitan Museum of Art) as well as the sentiment and hyperbole of Thomas Waterman Wood's *A Bit of War History: The Veteran* (1866; Metropolitan Museum of Art). During the Civil War, Inness had been an ardent Unionist and abolitionist, and he surely brought to his later veteran pictures a feeling for still-lingering sectional tensions.[40] *In the Gloaming/The Old Veteran* depicts the ever-apparent reality of aging, overworked, penniless, undernourished former soldiers of the Union and Confederacy—a situation of grave concern to the U.S. Pension Bureau and other government offices. Inness's hunched-over veteran reminds us of historian R. B. Rosenburg's

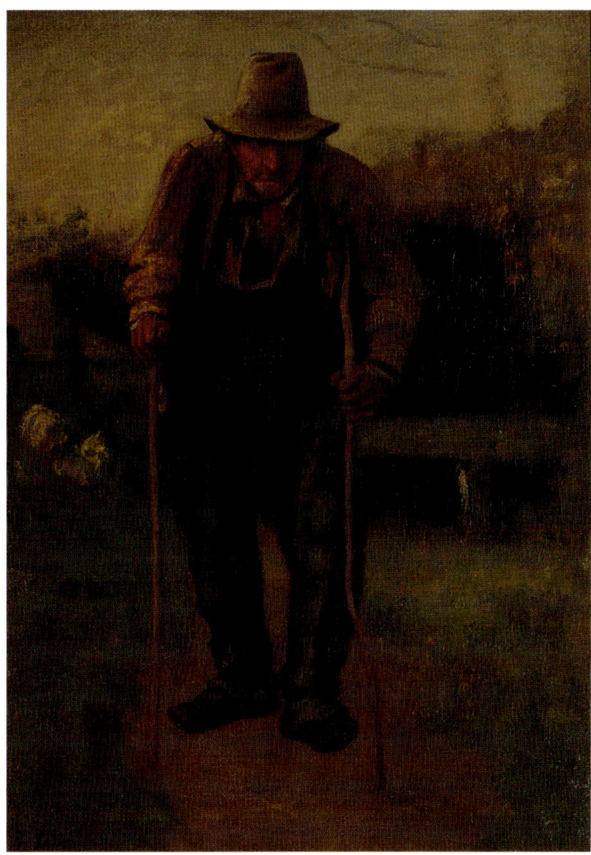

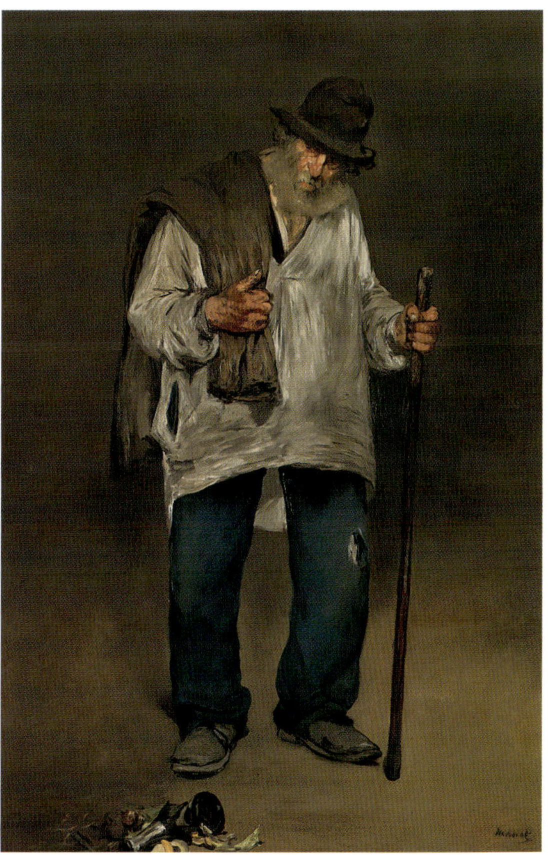

Figure 17
George Inness, *The Old Veteran*, ca. 1881, oil on canvas, 38½ x 26¼ inches. Montclair Art Museum. Gift of Mrs. Daniel J. Schuyler, 1953.70. IN EXHIBITION

Figure 18
Édouard Manet, *The Ragpicker*, ca. 1865–70, oil on canvas, 76¾ x 51½ inches. The Norton Simon Foundation.

observation that, in addition to ex-soldiers' other unhealed wounds, "the inability to stand upright without flinching had seriously curtailed a veteran's postwar economic activity."[41] Inness frequently flaunted his awareness of contemporary French painting, and, in suggesting an equation between old age, destitution, squalor, and decrepitude, he may well have sought prototypes in earlier figural pieces with similar themes of indigence, such as Édouard Manet's *The Ragpicker* (1865–70; fig. 18).[42]

The veteran in Inness's paintings has been identified as Lyman Beam, an ex-soldier Inness used as a model when he worked in Milton, New Jersey, in the early 1880s.[43] We know little else about Beam, but his soiled clothing and physical decay, intentionally or unwittingly, plays on popular, largely unfounded fears that veterans were dangerous, shifty, crime-prone outcasts.[44] Many Civil War veterans were in fact addicted to alcohol and opiates and suffered from what is today called post-traumatic stress disorder. The countenance of Inness's shadowy, disconsolate subject in turn recalls the readjustment issues faced by veterans of this or any war.[45]

The Arrears Act of 1879 greatly loosened and liberalized pension laws, and by 1885, 17 percent of Civil War veterans were receiving pensions, up from 2 percent in 1865 and 5 percent in 1870.[46] For a sense of the

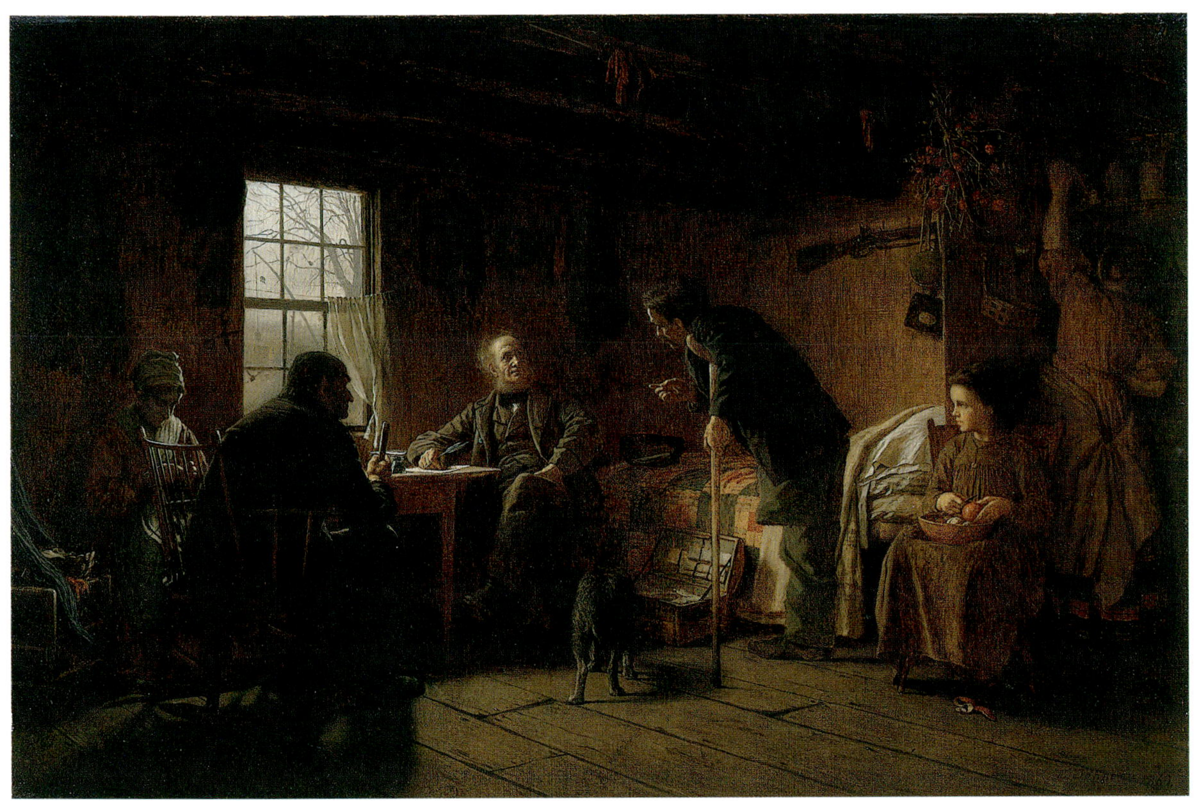

Figure 19
Eastman Johnson, *The Pension Claim Agent*, 1867, oil on canvas, 25¼ x 37⅜ inches. Fine Arts Museums of San Francisco. Museum purchase, Mildred Anna Williams Collection, 1943.6.
IN EXHIBITION

Figure 20 (opposite)
Jean François Millet, *The Gleaners*, 1857, oil on canvas, 32⅞ x 43¹¹⁄₁₆ inches. Musée d'Orsay, Paris, France. Inv.: RF 592. Photo: Jean Schormans. Réunion des Musées Nationaux/Art Resource, NY.

pension-granting mechanism in the earlier period, we might look to Eastman Johnson's *The Pension Claim Agent* (1867; fig. 19). Pictured in his simple farmhouse and surrounded by his family, the subject, who has lost a leg to battle or disease (or both), appeals to the older gentleman. During the war the government had begun assigning monetary value to the loss of specific limbs and biological functions. Johnson's painting captures the difficult process of applying for a pension in the pre–Arrears Act years as well as the potentially demoralizing matter of presenting a no-longer-existing leg as justification—corroboration—for compensation.[47] An observer of this scene likened the "humble room[,] which serves at once for kitchen, family meeting place, and bedroom" to "the crippled" and "mutilated soldier" himself. The same source emphasized the veteran's "sacrifice" and praised Johnson's "at once touching, dramatic, and thoroughly national composition" as "one of his signal triumphs of his career."[48] National trauma, bodily ruin, and financial hardship are at once romanticized, justified, and mollified in a stabilizing composition of modest but well-kept furnishings and muted blood-red tones.

In such a painting, the scale and location of the figures within the composition are often as important as the color and paint handling as means of

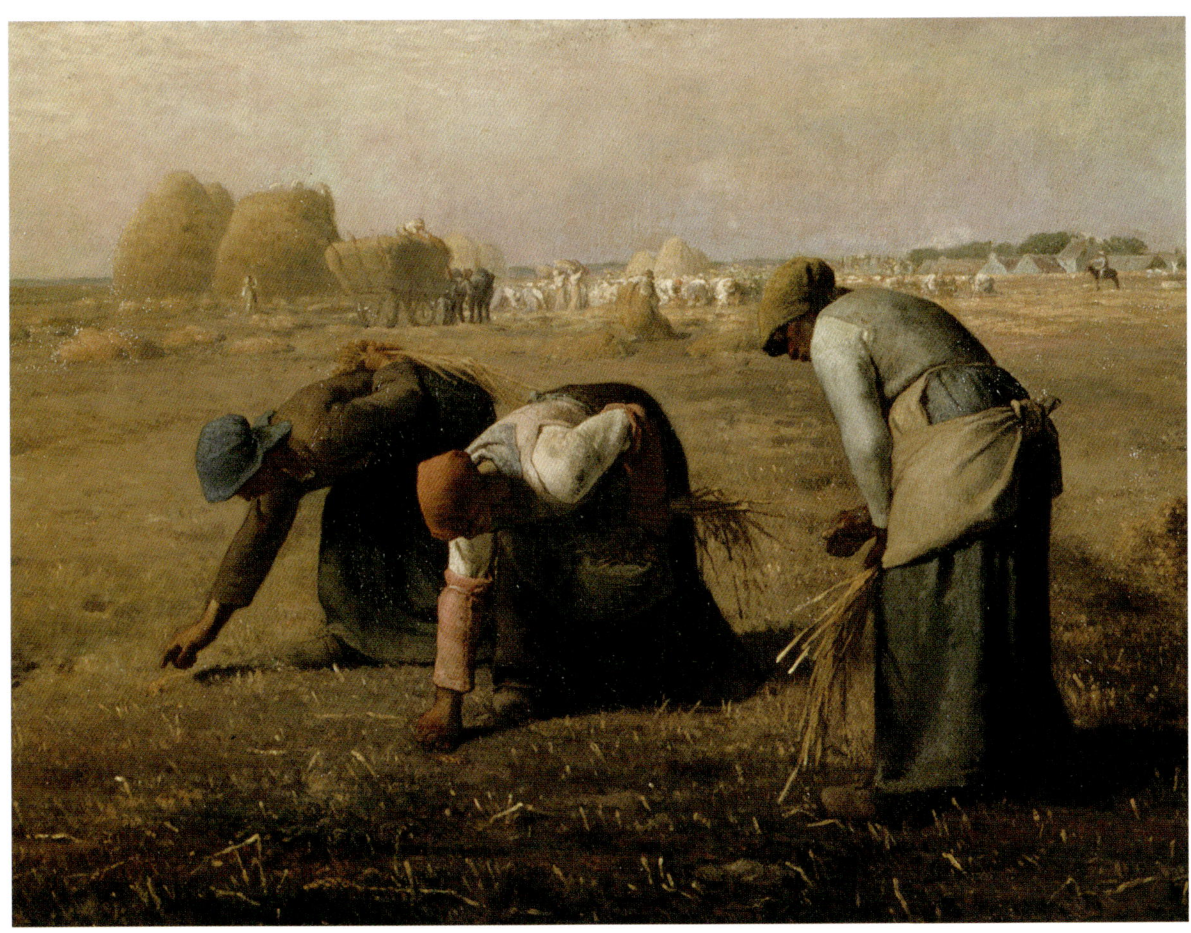

buffering the narrative and rendering it palatable. Consciously at times and probably unconsciously at others, artists of the era used these and other strategies and devices to offset and allay social problems, alluding to French academic and Barbizon meditations on labor, loss, and hardship. As art historian T. J. Clark pointed out in *The Absolute Bourgeois*, Jean-François Millet's peasant landscape paintings appealed to conservative nineteenth-century French audiences precisely because they presented mind-numbing drudgery at safe remove. In pictures like *The Gleaners* (1857), the artist neutralized the exertion and gloom of manual labor by placing figures just far enough into the middle ground to situate agricultural toil at a "decent distance" (fig. 20).[49] In searching for prototypes of what we might call the taxing gaze in American art, and the buffering distance it can command, Millet is an important figure to consider. In late nineteenth-century American art, literary criticism, and the radical and popular press alike, the French artist was frequently held up as a standard according to which painters could depict laborers and the destitute with a sort of dignity.[50] Among Millet's most fervent

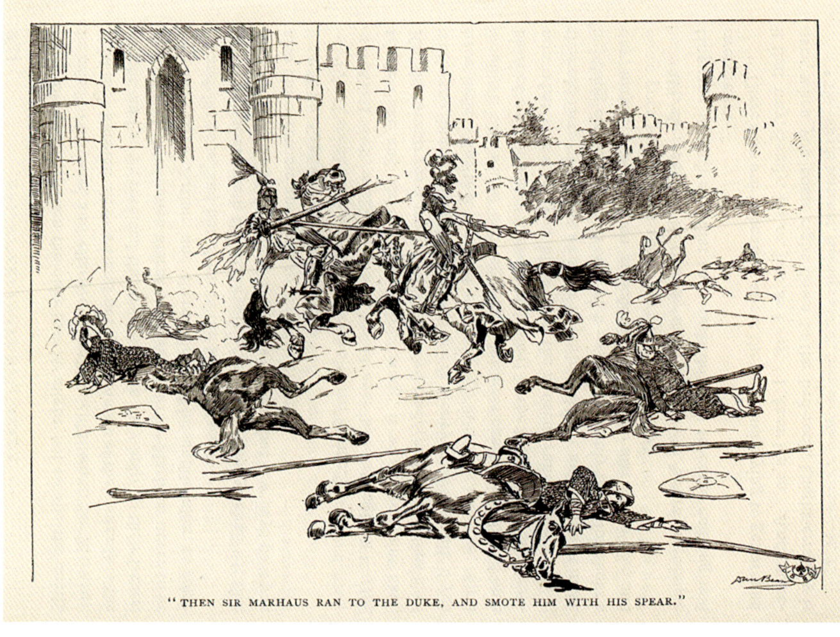

"THEN SIR MARHAUS RAN TO THE DUKE, AND SMOTE HIM WITH HIS SPEAR."

Figure 21
Daniel Carter Beard, *"Then Sir Marhaus Ran to the Duke, and Smote Him With His Spear,"* engraving in Mark Twain, *A Connecticut Yankee in King Arthur's Court* (New York: C. L. Webster & Company, 1889). Special Collections Library, The Pennsylvania State University Libraries, University Park, Pennsylvania.
IN EXHIBITION

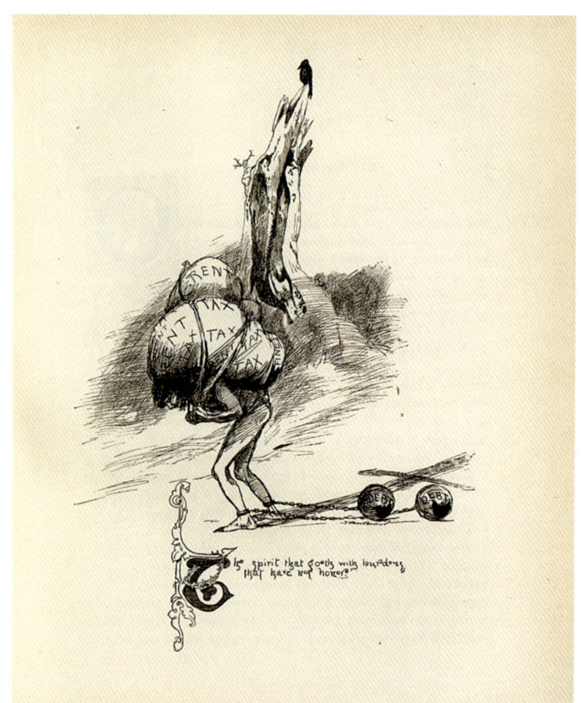

Figure 22
Daniel Carter Beard, *"The spirit that goeth with burdens that have not honor,"* engraving in Mark Twain, *A Connecticut Yankee in King Arthur's Court* (New York: C. L. Webster & Company, 1889). Special Collections Library, The Pennsylvania State University Libraries, University Park, Pennsylvania.

American admirers was Inness, who used a similar toil-neutralizing formula in such works as *Peace and Plenty* (1865; Metropolitan Museum of Art).[51]

There are of course other ways in which the "distance" becomes palatable and "decent," and the vision less taxing. The lens of time, for instance, also offered a useful buffer against the unseemliness of financial hardship. Easel painters, muralists, and illustrators—like several contemporary writers—were especially lured by medieval history and faux-medieval lore, particularly King Arthur literature. Medievalizing artists and authors grafted upon nineteenth-century America a past of innocence, sincerity, purpose, and, often, mystical insight. Equally important, these individuals found in the medieval a vehicle through which to understand and critique Reconstruction-era and Gilded Age socioeconomic turmoil.[52]

Daniel Carter Beard, one of the most famous illustrators of the period, became especially renowned for his illustrations of Mark Twain's novel *A Connecticut Yankee in King Arthur's Court* (1889), perhaps the most famous example of medievalism in American literature. An avid Single Taxer from early on, Beard brought to his art a linear finesse that he used to wage piquant satire and pose trenchant ironies.[53] His illustrations for

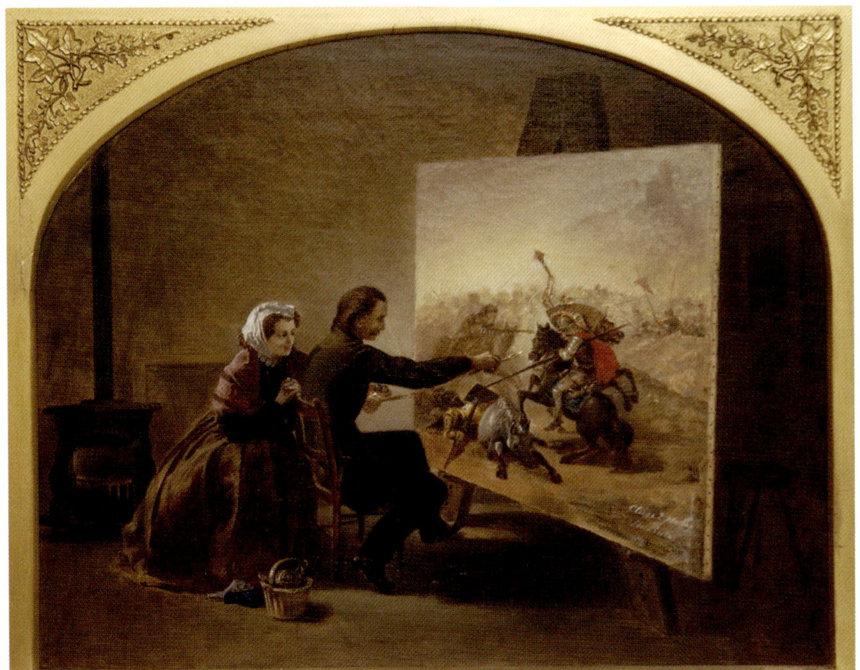

Figure 23
John Harrison Mills, *Artist Painting a Satirical Painting*, ca. 1870s–80s, oil on canvas, 20 x 24½ inches. Collection of Jean and Alvin Snowiss.
IN EXHIBITION

Connecticut Yankee cloak a scathing critique of money's ills and bloated greed in a generic, often gory, visual language of armor, lances, knights, and jousts, as seen in *"Then Sir Marhaus ran to the duke, and smote him with his spear"* (fig. 21). In a few instances, however, Beard collapsed the buffer of time and place, as in an illustration of a feudal slave driver who is a not-so-veiled likeness of robber baron Jay Gould.[54] In keeping with other American illustrators, Beard on occasion included words such as "free trade," "rent," "tax," "fines," and "property" to dispel any narrative confusion. In *"The spirit that goeth with burdens that have not honor,"* he inscribed this language on the bags and chained ankle weights impeding the figure's progress, with visual stereotypes of medieval chivalry damning the character of one who could impose such burdens (fig. 22). Illustrations like Beard's, occupying an intersection of cultural and economic interests, merit close attention in the study of taxing visions because so many ideals and vernacular metaphors regarding property, value, and inequity were codified in popular periodicals and fiction. Moreover, as the examples of narrative (and occasionally medievalizing) artists such as Maxfield Parrish, Howard Pyle, and N. C. Wyeth would make clear by the early twentieth century, the categories of high art and literary illustration could and often did overlap.

In contrast to the gothic follies and medieval lore of Parrish and Wyeth, or the stylized exaggerations of Beard, John Harrison Mills's *Artist Painting a Satirical Painting* (ca. 1870s–80s) offers a more subtle—if equally potent—example of the force of the medieval on a mindset that sought a condensed

Figure 24
John Harrison Mills, *Artist Painting a Satirical Painting*, ca. 1870s–80s, detail of fig. 23.

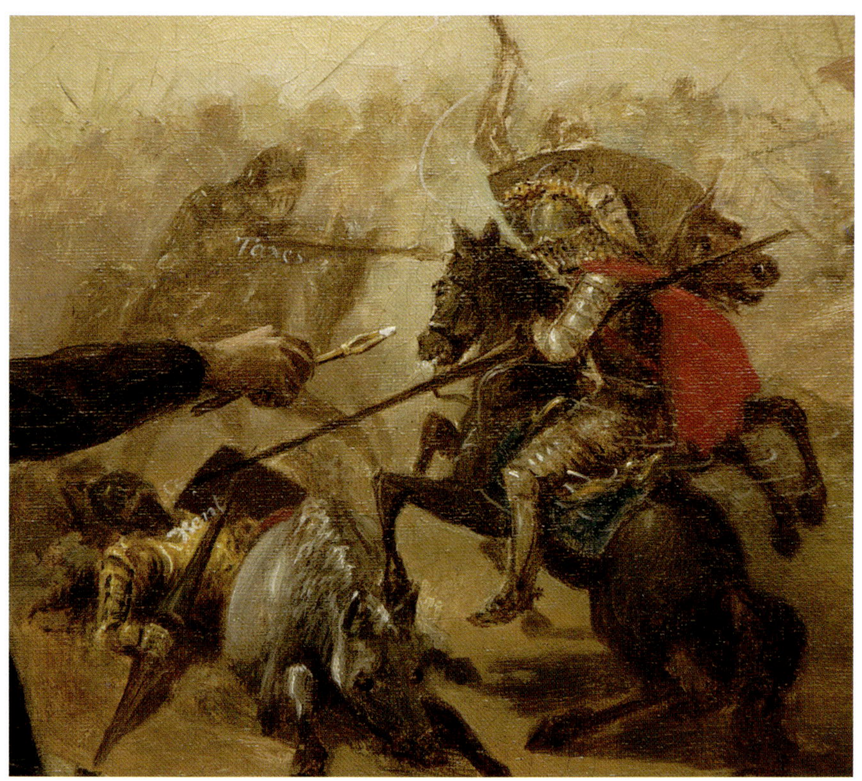

Figure 25 (opposite)
Henry Hutt, *My Dear Kate, You Have No Idea How Hard Put to It I Am to Make Ends Meet. I Am So Poor It Is a Scandal*, 1899, gouache on illustration board, $25\frac{13}{16}$ x $29\frac{7}{8}$ inches. Delaware Art Museum. Acquisition Fund, 1983.
IN EXHIBITION

and occasionally diluted form of social critique (fig. 23). Mills, too, envisions a "usable past" offered by way of some distant, feudal—if fictional—yesterday. The case of Mills is also worth recounting in some detail because it suggests parallels between easel painting and the popular press and literary illustration. Wounded at the Second Battle of Bull Run (1862), Mills found work after the war as an artist-correspondent for the *Buffalo Express*. From August 1869 through January 1871, Mark Twain also worked at the *Express*, and it was probably there that the men met.[55] Significantly, Twain's first column for the newspaper—his "Salutatory"—complained bitterly about the recently instituted federal income tax. In telling his readers what they might expect from him, he promised he would not curse, although, he added, the subject of taxation might test him: "I . . . shall never use profanity except in discussing house-rent and taxes."[56] The imposition of a federal income tax in 1863 was bitterly contested, and it was extensively reported and debated in the *Express* and throughout the national press for years to come.[57]

Artist Painting a Satirical Painting critiques the controversial topic of taxation. Just to the right of a wood stove in a dimly lit studio, a fashionably dressed woman clasps her hands on a chair where an artist sits, apparently making finishing touches to a painting of a medieval battle. In the foreground of the canvas on the easel, a red-caped knight directs his spear at a similarly clad fallen figure, on whose chest is inscribed, "Rent." Partly obscured by the large, centrally placed knight is another man on horseback, on whose raised spear is written "Bills" (fig. 24). An additional rider, with the word "Taxes" on his chest, charges from the left, jabbing his lance into the red-caped knight, who may be seen as the hero warding off the evil triumvirate of rent, bills, and taxes. Mills has enlisted medieval imagery to wage his social commentary in much the same way Twain would in *A Connecticut Yankee*.[58] As we have seen, Beard used similar strategies in his illustrations for Twain. *Artist Painting a Satirical Painting* shares with *"Then Sir Marhaus ran to the duke"* a delight and catharsis in unadulterated violence, even using similar positions for such details as the lances and the horses on hind legs (see fig. 21). Somewhat remarkably, both men inscribe their art with pecuniary words (see fig. 22). Rather than one artist directly influencing the other, it is more likely the case that Mills and Beard were both aware of the standard visual tropes of not only American medievalism but also socioeconomic satire.

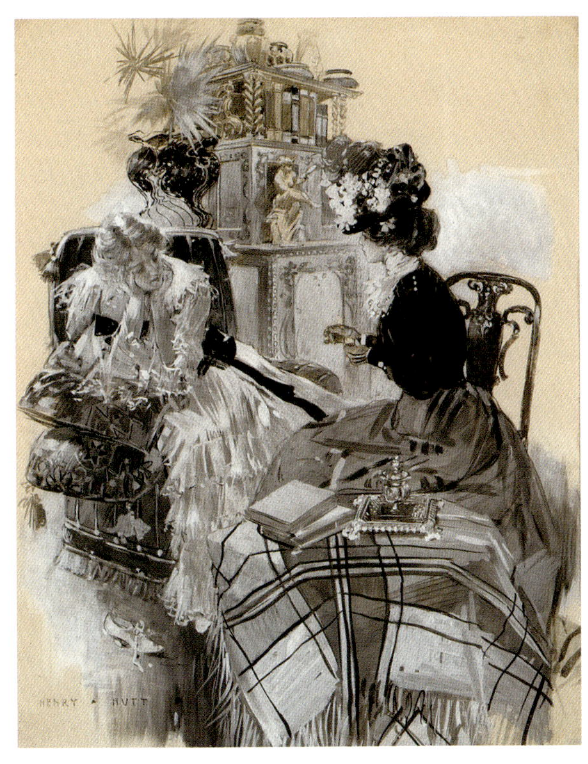

American authors and illustrators in later nineteenth-century popular magazines also reckoned with the buffering distance between comfort and poverty in more conventional ways. Particularly noteworthy is the case of the illustrator Henry Hutt, who provided drawings for *Ladies' Home Journal*, *McClure's*, *Life*, and the *Saturday Evening Post*. An early piece by the artist accompanying the short story "Wanted: A Chaperon" graced the cover of the *Saturday Evening Post* on April 15, 1899, and appeared later that year in the author Mrs. Burton Harrison's book *The Carcellini, with Other Tales* (fig. 25).[59] Depicting the "childless young widow of a naval officer," Gwendolyn West, in her opulent parlor, telling her woes to her friend Kate Payne, the drawing takes its title from the text: *"My dear Kate, you have no idea how hard put to it I am to make ends meet. I am so poor it is a scandal"* (1899). "If my Aunt Althea had not invested her money in this flat, when the house was going up," Gwendolyn confides in Kate, "I should be living in one room of a boarding-house, with a folding bed." Hutt envelops the figure in floral arrangements, richly brocaded fabrics, and imported French furniture. The loosely applied gouache, delicate lines, and cascading forms bespeak Gwendolyn's precious world, well buffered from the dreaded lower-class living arrangements she is only one unpaid bill away from occupying.[60] "Status-striving," historian Jackson Lears has recently noted, was "responsible for busting many a family budget" in Gilded Age and Progressive era America.[61] Hutt's picture in turn suggests a correlation between the overflowing bric-a-brac and Gwendolyn's present predicament.

Even when her maid and cook threaten to leave because of her mounting insolvency, Gwendolyn cannot concentrate; she can think only of Kate's suggestion that she chaperone some young woman whom she might make "picturesque," with whom she might tour through France and Italy, "far from the sound of trolley cars and tokens of a city's overcrowded life that, day or night, can never be hushed!" Gwendolyn, that is, wants some distance from the diurnal realities of New York. Most important, at present she needs money—and she expects to be well paid for being a chaperone. After all, she reminds Kate, "With a full purse you can accomplish wonders."[62] A full purse, Hutt's illustration suggests, makes possible the creature comforts with which she might sulk, contemplate, and otherwise transcend her immediate time and place. Gwendolyn may not yet be in Italy, but the vase with palm fronds, the Renaissance-style secretary topped with urns, the statuette of a Narcissus figure admiring itself in the mirror, and the Scottish tartan cloth over the table (replete with card-receiving tray) all work to transport Gwendolyn somewhere far from her present financial straits in America.

As one might imagine, the psychic and physical distance enjoyed by Gwendolyn was largely off-limits to African Americans and other non-Caucasians. Their circumstances, of course, were in many cases precisely what provoked the recurring Gwendolyn archetype to seek a buffer and palliative. Following the debacle of Reconstruction, as the federal government withdrew its active promotion and protection of African Americans in civic life, racism escalated, often in the form of lynching, and several additional measures banned non-Caucasians from "the parade of economic progress."[63] Some paintings of the period depict African Americans as one among so many types—along with the elderly, the rural, animals, women, and so on—relegated to the sidelines of the national parade. But even in pictures that survey an inventory of types, such as Henry's *Capital and Labor*, the African American frequently appears unable—too young, too undeveloped—to participate in a burgeoning capitalist economy (see fig. 12). Children (probably brothers) also occupy Hal Alexander Courtney Morrison's painting *Weighing the Cotton* (1885–90; see fig. 47). The title and subject matter refer to the Atlanta-based artist's encounters with sharecroppers in the post-Reconstruction South. The best the children can do, this painting suggests, is to sell off their profits for rent. The child is a cog in a larger, bitter system.[64]

Joining the African American child as a wholesale sign of unrealized potential or financial obsolescence is the tottering, elderly, dark-skinned figure who so frequently symbolized not only monetary hardship but also physical incapacity. This is the case with a small group of paintings by Alfred Kappes depicting some aged African Americans conversing and paying their house

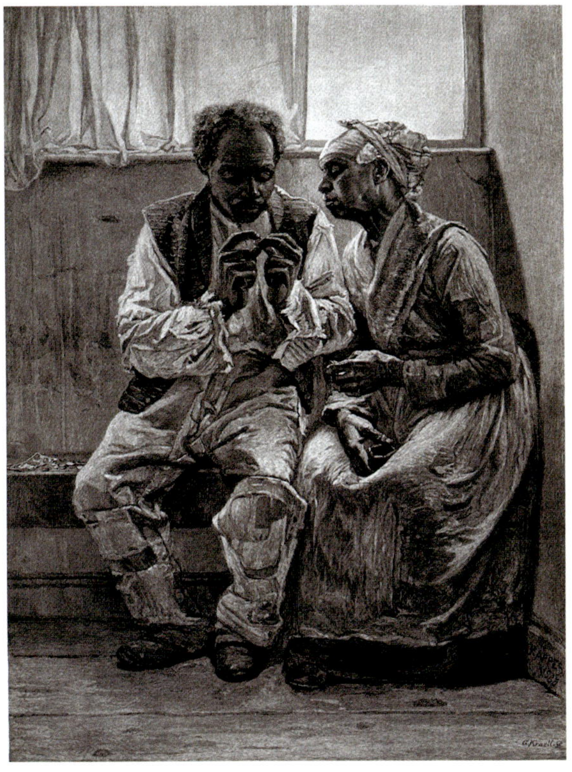

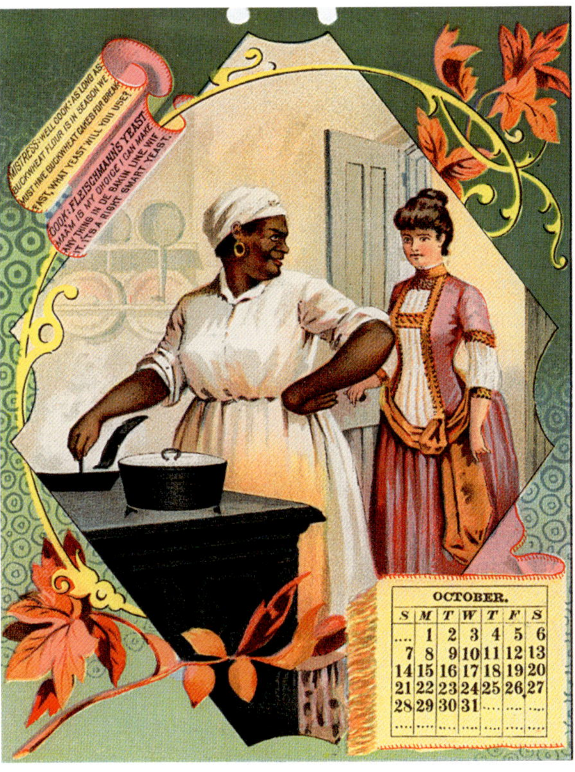

rent within a domestic or perhaps administrative setting. The artist's *Rent Day* (1887), known today only from a wood engraving, shows a husband and wife counting and otherwise examining their money; coins and paper lay on the bench at left, with the small purse on the woman's lap a sign of their modest circumstances (fig. 26). A biography of the artist in the catalogue published upon the liquidation in 1899 of patron Thomas B. Clarke's American art collection—Clarke owned *Rent Day*—notes Kappes's reputation for pictures of "touching and sad significance." Enlisting a condescending, racist vocabulary typical of the period, the catalogue entry for the painting states, "The [rent] agent has made his monthly call at the humble habitation of Sambo and Dinah." (The reproduction of the print after *Rent Day*, shown here as it appeared in William MacKay Laffan's book, *Engravings on Wood* [1887], crops out the agent at left).[65]

In the evolving visual mythology of demeaning African stereotypes, Sambo signified a childishly humorous, unthreateningly lazy man, while Dinah connoted an indefatigably mirthful, nurturing, typically full-bodied woman who lived to serve others.[66] Firmly locating Kappes's figure in the Dinah/Mammy camp is the madras head wrap, which appeared in numerous advertisements and popular illustrations (fig. 27). "On her best days," wrote Harriet Beecher Stowe of the Dinah figure in *Uncle Tom's Cabin*, she "dress[ed] herself up in a smart dress, clean apron, and high, brilliant

Figure 26
Gustave Kruell, after Alfred Kappes, *Rent Day*, 1887, engraving, 15½ x 12¼ inches. In William MacKay Laffan, *Engravings on Wood, by Members of the Society of American Engravers* (New York: Harper & Brothers, 1887), n.p. The Huntington Library, Art Collections, and Botanical Gardens.
IN EXHIBITION

Figure 27
Fleischman's Yeast trade card, 1880s. Warshaw Collection of Business Americana—Yeast, Archives Center, National Museum of American History, Behring Center, Smithsonian Institution.

Figure 28
Alfred Kappes, *Tattered and Torn*, 1886, oil on canvas, 40 x 32 inches. Smith College Museum of Art, Northampton, Massachusetts. Purchased with the Beatrice Oenslager Chace, class of 1928, Fund, the Rita Rich Fraad, class of 1937, Fund for American Art, the Kathleen Compton Sherrerd, class of 1954, Fund for American Art, and with restricted acquisition funds.
IN EXHIBITION

Figure 29 (opposite)
Thomas Waterman Wood, *Crossing the Ferry*, 1878, watercolor, 18¾ x 26¼ inches. T. W. Wood Gallery and Arts Center, Montpelier, Vermont.
IN EXHIBITION

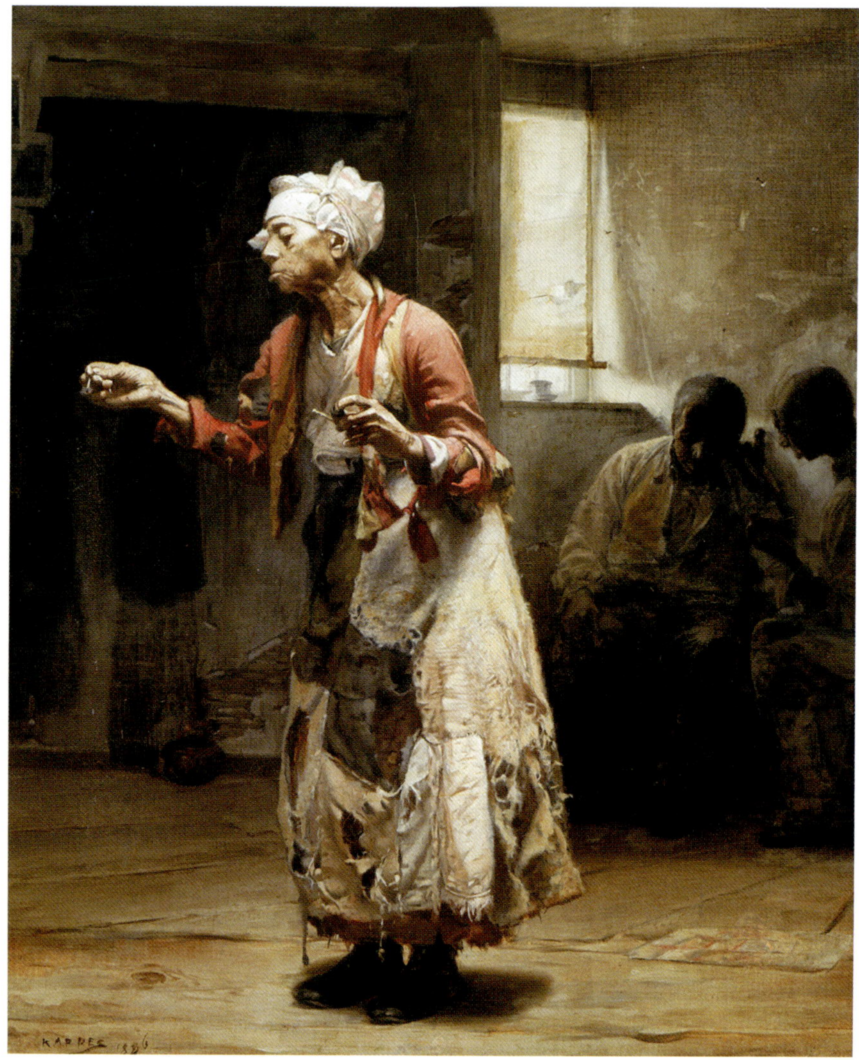

turban."[67] Kappes's domestic servant appears again in the painting *Tattered and Torn* (1886), bearing the same facial features, arthritic hands, and turban seen in *Rent Day* (fig. 28). The former painting is almost the exact size of *Rent Day*, features the same woman-in-profile, and positions the figures on a bench by a window (as a few other works in this series do). The paintings appear to be pendants, different parts of the same rent-paying narrative, as if that saga has been slowed down to an almost unbearably protracted tempo. Having lost her apron, and so decrepit she can barely light her pipe, the woman in *Tattered and Torn* reveals her frayed and dilapidated rag-patched dress. Many Americans—especially racist and nativist groups like the burgeoning Ku Klux Klan—saw signs of threat, revolution, and transgression in the financially ambitious and successful African American.[68] Kappes's paintings, though they depict the seamy underside of financial indigence, suggest there is little to worry about, only a spectacle of poverty held at a distance.

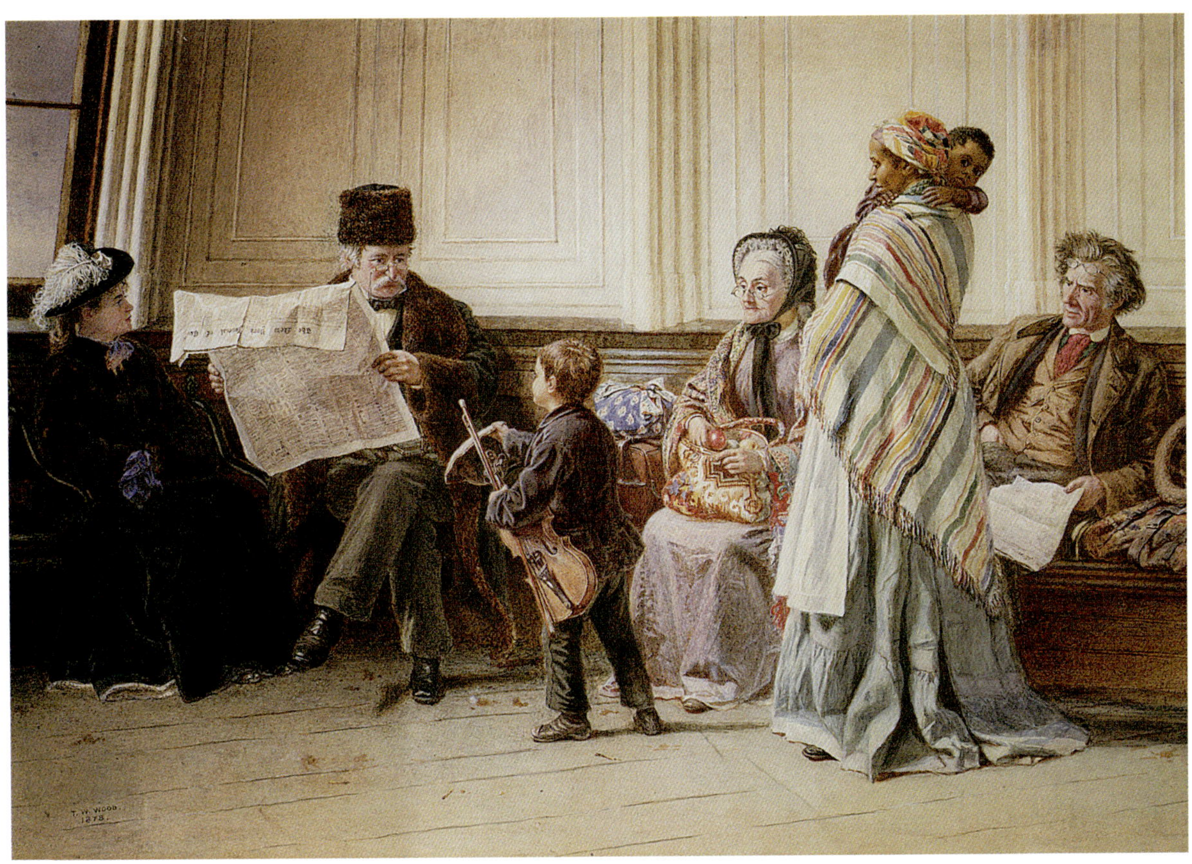

Closer to the Dinah/Mammy figure is the African American mother and child at right in Thomas Waterman Wood's watercolor *Crossing the Ferry* (1878), where, again, the woman wears the servitude-denoting madras wrap (fig. 29).[69] If her ebullience is muted by her turned back, it is amplified by her brightly colored outfit and the cuddly child who meets our gaze. Most remarkable, however, is her *reason* for looking elsewhere: not unlike the newspaper reader wearing a paphuka hat at left, she witnesses the musician-waif's appeal operating at full throttle, as if Anglo cuteness and sentiment are somehow worthier of alms and attention, more easily converted into cash, than those of Africans and African Americans. She watches the white child as the elderly woman to her left reaches into her purse, and the gentleman at right lifts up his spectacles, puts down his newspaper, and mines his pants pocket for money for the boy violinist. The African American child, meanwhile, gazes elsewhere, perhaps to sites beyond the picture plane, perhaps to the artist or implied beholder.

In later nineteenth-century American visual culture, when older African Americans *do* engage the market economy, it is often somewhat on the sly, in marginal fashion, as in Stanley Fox's illustration *Evading the Excise Law—Laying in Rum for Sunday*, which appeared on the front page of *Harper's Weekly* early in 1868 (fig. 30). "Nowhere and at no time," notes the

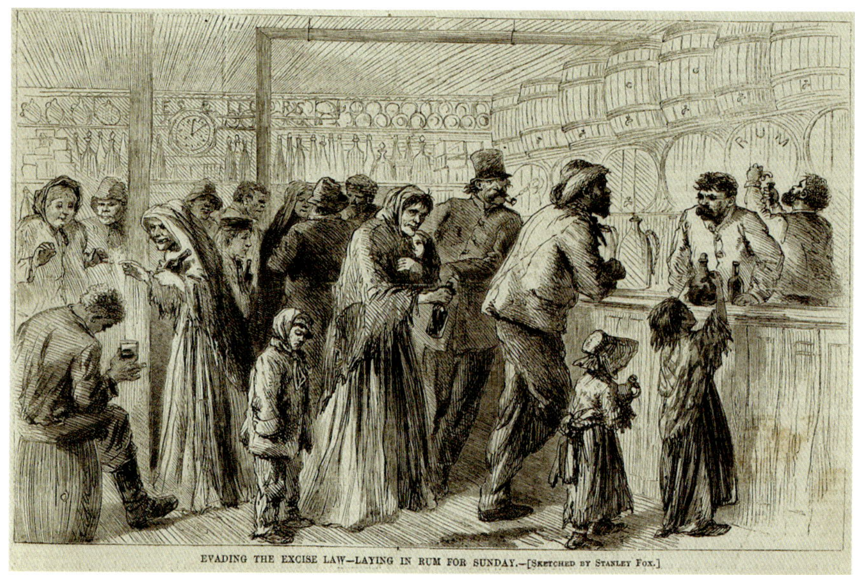

Figure 30
Stanley Fox, *Evading the Excise Law—Laying in Rum for Sunday*, engraving in *Harper's Weekly Magazine* 11, February 6, 1867, p. 1. The Pennsylvania State University Libraries, University Park, Pennsylvania.
IN EXHIBITION

text accompanying Fox's engraving, "will a person behold more squalor, degradation, and misery than in a New York rum-shop on any Saturday evening."[70] At the front of the rum shop line are an African American man and (presumably) his two ragamuffin children. In the logic of the *Harper's* column, they stand at the forefront of the cast of depraved types. But the viewer, the magazine reader, need not actually "behold" this vice-in-action; the magazine presents the desperation of Saturday alcohol purchases as news, as something of a revelation (even though for many readers it surely was not news). For all their documentary realism, profusely illustrated periodicals such as *Harper's* and *Frank Leslie's* often provided the very distance that transformed documentation into illustration, taxing episodes into those worth reading about and engaging visually.

In the early twenty-first century—as in the late nineteenth—artists continue to both document and critique taxing visions, reckoning with the proximity of visual pleasure to pecuniary reality. And now as then, at stake is nothing less than the distance an artist, patron, beholder, or visual subject may construct between these two realms. One thinks of the work of, among other artists, Sandow Birk, Phillip Hefferton, Erika Rothenberg, Sue Coe, Kerry James Marshall, and George Segal. Offering a particularly useful meditation on the gap between taxing visions and the rarefied pictorial settings in which they appear are the paintings and prints of Enrique Chagoya. In *An Illegal Alien's Guide to the Theory of Surplus Value* (2009), a Brazilian woman wearing the recurring African head wrap looms large upon a port replete with both functioning and incapacitated freighters (fig. 31). As in so many taxing visions, however, the bust is relegated to a nonthreatening background. Recalling Mills's and Beard's medievalizing imagery, much

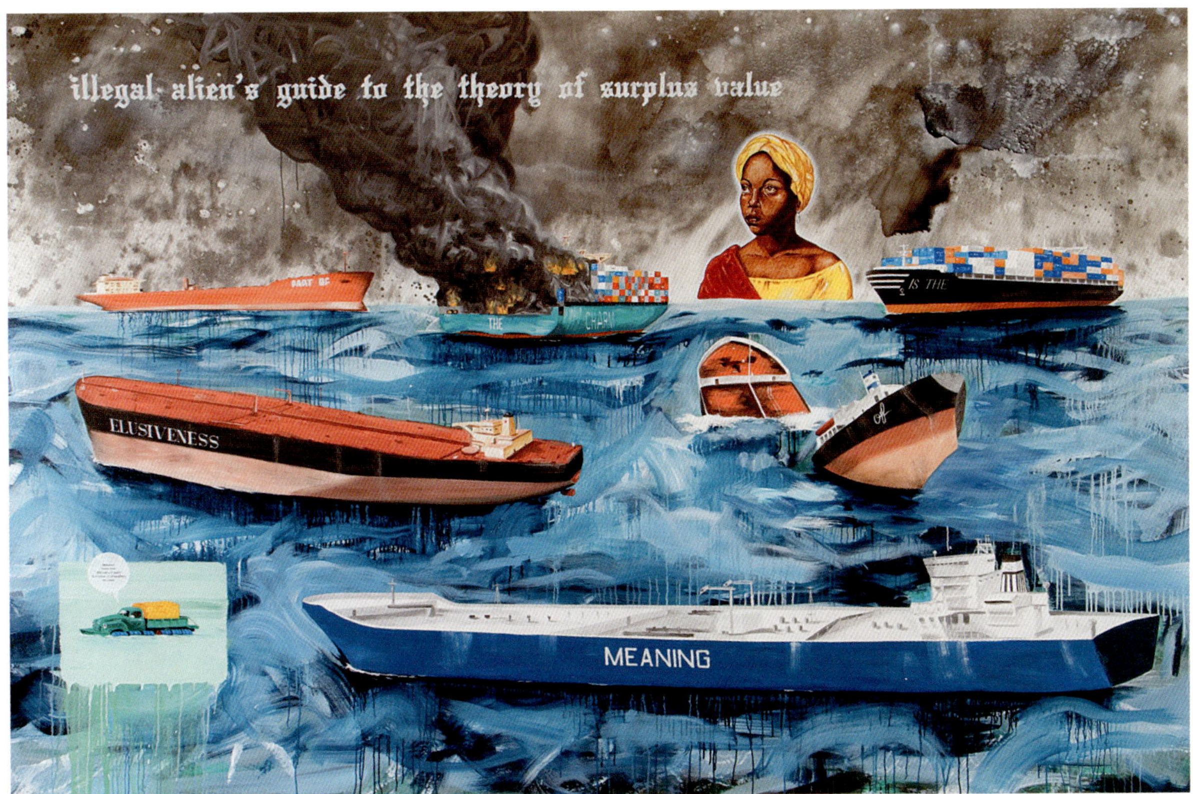

Figure 31
Enrique Chagoya, *An Illegal Alien's Guide to the Theory of Surplus Value*, 2009, acrylic and water-based oil on canvas, 80 x 120 inches. © Enrique Chagoya. Courtesy of George Adams Gallery, New York.

of the meaning here is carried by the artist's inscriptions (see figs. 21–24). Chagoya wrote the title text in the sky with a black letter (although here whitened) German typeface, perhaps reminding us that the line comes from Karl Marx's three-volume *Theories of Surplus Value* (1862–63), which would eventually form part of the author's *Capital*.[71]

On the sides of the ships is yet more text, forming the sentence, "Part of the charm is the elusiveness of meaning." Whatever else Chagoya evokes here, figuring prominently is the sense that underlying meanings (of trade, of business, of art, of ideas) can get lost or muddled when subjected to the socially sanctioned, market-dictated vagaries of painterly "charm." As we have seen, for Whistler and many of his followers, the collapse of subject matter—in favor of rarefied form itself—provided the ameliorating buffer between ourselves and the Venetian beggars or the girls looking longingly into a Chelsea shop window. In the poem "Burnt Norton" from the *Four Quartets* (1943), T. S. Eliot made the perhaps obvious but nonetheless sobering comment, "Humankind cannot bear very much reality."[72] From John George Brown to Eliot to Chagoya, artists past and present have alternately aestheticized poverty—whether on North Atherton Street, in New York, or in Venice—and dismantled the distance between that reality and ourselves.

1. Mike Joseph, "Nowhere Else to Go," *Centre Daily Times*, August 27, 2006, p. 1, and "Squeezed Out—The Residents of a North Atherton Trailer Park Will Have to Find Another Place to Call Home as Development Plans Move Forward," *Centre Daily Times*, November 7, 2006, p. 1; Jennifer Thomas, "Retail Center Gets Mobile-Home Land," *Centre Daily Times*, June 14, 2006, p. 9. On land tenure, social stigma, the swiftness of eviction and park dissolution, and the impact of zoning on mobile home residents, see Destiny D. Aman and Brent Yarnal, "Home Sweet Mobile Home? Benefits and Challenges of Mobile Home Ownership in Rural Pennsylvania," *Applied Geography* 30 (January 2010): 84–95, esp. 85–86.

2. Aman and Yarnal, "Home Sweet Mobile Home?" 86.

3. Elizabeth Johns's groundbreaking volume *American Genre Painting: The Politics of Everyday Life* (New Haven: Yale University Press, 1991) and Sarah Burns's equally important book *Painting the Dark Side, Art and the Gothic Imagination in Nineteenth-Century America* (Berkeley: University of California Press, 2004) deal with inequity as subject matter and relentlessly probe just whose "everyday" selected genre paintings purport to depict.

4. Vincent DiGirolamo, "Newsboy Funerals: Tales of Sorrow and Solidarity in Urban America," *Journal of Social History* 36, no. 1 (2002): 7.

5. On Cafferty, see David Stewart Hull, *James Henry Cafferty* (New York: New-York Historical Society, 1986); and Wendy J. Katz, "Fancy Painting, Street Children, and the Fast Men of the Pavé," *Nineteenth-Century Studies* 21 (2007): 85–126.

6. T. Allston Brown, *A History of the New York Stage from the First Performance in 1732 to 1901*, 3 vols. (New York: Dodd, Mead and Company, 1903), 1:137.

7. Richard M. Dorson, *America in Legend: Folklore from the Colonial Period to the Present* (New York: Pantheon Books, 1973), 102.

8. See Edward T. O'Donnell and Henry Lee, "From Engine 40: Mose," *New York Daily News*, March 5, 2002, news section, p. 31.

9. For Brown, see Martha J. Hoppin, *Country Paths and City Sidewalks: The Art of John George Brown* (Springfield, Mass.: George Walter Vincent Smith Art Museum, 1989); and Claire Perry, *Young America: Childhood in 19th-Century Art and Culture* (New Haven: Yale University Press, in association with Iris and Gerald B. Cantor Center for Visual Arts, Stanford University, 2006), 136–41. Also very helpful is Lisa N. Peters, "Images of the Homeless in American Art, 1860–1910," in Rick Beard, ed., *On Being Homeless: Historical Perspectives* (New York: Museum of the City of New York, 1988), 42–67.

10. John Wilmerding, *An American Perspective: Nineteenth-Century Art from the Collection of Jo Ann & Julian Ganz, Jr.* (Washington, D.C.: National Gallery of Art, 1981), 53. Peters, "Images of the Homeless," 52. I am grateful to Joan Adler of the Straus Historical Society for sharing with me documentation of Isidor Straus's patronage of John George Brown and other artists in the 1890s (e-mail correspondence, July 24, 2009).

11. "The Name Makes the Picture," *New York Times*, April 10, 1886, p. 8.

12. Viviana A. Zelizer, *The Social Meaning of Money: Pin Money, Paychecks, Poor Relief, and Other Currencies* (New York: Basic Books, 1994), 143–69.

13. For Gilded Age and Progressive era floral-female painting, see Annette Stott, "Floral Femininity: A Pictorial Definition," *American Art* 6 (Spring 1992): 60–77.

14. *Oxford English Dictionary*, s.v. "posy."

15. Anne Beuning, Cincinnati Art Museum, e-mail correspondence with author, June 10, 2009.

16. For Mosler, see Barbara C. Gilbert, *Henry Mosler Rediscovered: A Nineteenth-Century American-Jewish Artist* (Los Angeles: Skirball Museum/Skirball Cultural Center, 1995). My thanks to art historian Clarence Burton Sheffield Jr. for alerting me to the significance of bunads in late nineteenth-century Paris.

17. William Gerdts, "The Empty Room," *Allen Memorial Art Museum Bulletin* 33, no. 2 (1975–76): 82. On the artist more generally, see Gerdts, *Louis Moeller, N.A. (1855–1930): A Victorian Man's World* (New York: Grand Central Art Galleries, 1984).

18. [John Davis], "Louis Henry Charles Moeller," in David B. Dearinger, ed., *Painting and Sculpture in the Collection of the National Academy of Design*, vol. 1: 1826–1925 (New York: Hudson Hills Press, 2004), 396.

19. "Obituary. James Henry Cafferty, N.A.," *New York Herald*, September 9, 1869, p. 4.

20. George Inness, quoted in George Inness Jr., *Life, Art, and Letters of George Inness* (1917; New York: Dutton, 1931), 132, 151–52, 155.

21. Gerdts, "The Empty Room," 85.

22. Daniel T. Rodgers, *The Work Ethic in Industrial America, 1850–1920* (Chicago: University of Chicago Press, 1978), 55. Inness made a similar arrangement in the mid-1870s with Boston dealer Doll and Richards, which would ultimately sue the artist, with Inness countersuing on the grounds of misrepresentation or "wrongful conversion"; Nicolai Cikovsky Jr., "The Life and Work of George Inness" (PhD diss., Harvard University, 1965; reprint, New York: Garland Publishing, 1977), 56–59; Inness quoted in Cikovsky, *George Inness* (New York: Harry N. Abrams, 1993), 79.

23. Moeller produced a few other paintings of wills, including *Signing the Will*, [date unconfirmed], reproduced in *Fine Arts Journal* 23 (March 1910): 141; and *Reading the Will*, 1888, reproduced in *American Paintings, Drawings, and Sculpture*, auction catalogue, Sotheby's, New York, May 21, 2003, lot 213.

24. On Henry's "bifurcating" compositions, see Amy Kurtz Lansing, *Historical Fictions: Edward Lamson Henry's Paintings of Past and Present* (New Haven: Yale University Art Gallery, 2005), 36. A contemporary account interpreted the woman at right as a visitor to the "back porch of a farmhouse"; "Fine Arts: Studio Notes," *New York Herald*, November 14, 1881, p. 5.

25. "Notes of Art Work," *New York Daily Tribune*, November 27, 1881, p. 5; I am grateful to Amy Kurtz Lansing for directing me to this article and the one cited in n.24.

26. http://www.gutenberg.org/files/27327/27327-h/27327-h.htm. Sally McMurry, e-mail correspondence with author, November 18, 2009. Daryl Heasley, interview with author, January 21, 2010. Heasley is curator of the Pasto Agricultural Museum at The Pennsylvania State University.

27. "Fine Arts: Studio Notes," p. 5.

28. Christine Ammer, *The American Heritage Dictionary of Idioms* (New York: Houghton Mifflin, 1997), 722; William A. Craigie and James R. Hurlbert, *A Dictionary of American English on Historical Principles*, 4 vols. (Chicago: University of Chicago Press, 1938–44), 1:505.

29. Henry, quoted in Lansing, *Historical Fictions*, 25–26; see also p. 21.

30. Eric Denker, *Whistler and His Circle in Venice* (London: Merrell, 2003), 11–13. See also David Park Curry, *James McNeill Whistler: Uneasy Pieces* (Richmond: Virginia Museum of Fine Arts, 2004), 383.

31. Margaret F. MacDonald, *Palaces in the Night: Whistler in Venice* (Berkeley: University of California Press, 2001), 19–20; Ruth E. Fine, *Drawing Near: Whistler Etchings from the Zelman Collection* (Los Angeles: Los Angeles County Museum of Art, 1984), 21–22.

32. Alastair Grieve, "The Sites of Whistler's Venice Etchings," *Print Quarterly* 13 (March 1996): 25.

33. "Mr. Whistler's Pastels at the Fine Art Society," *London Standard*, February 1881, quoted in Curry, *James McNeill Whistler*, 383.

34. On the Chelsea scenes, see Britt Salvesen, "The Streets of London," *Art Institute of Chicago Museum Studies* 24, no. 1 (1998): 44–53; and Curry, *James McNeill Whistler*, 288–93.

35. See John Fowles, *A Short History of Lyme Regis* (Boston: Little, Brown and Company, 1982), 43, 48; and Barbara Kerr, *Bound to the Soil: A Social History of Dorset, 1750–1918* (London: John Baker Publishers, 1968), 99–100.

36. Curry, *James McNeill Whistler*; Marc Simpson, ed., *Like Breath on Glass: Whistler,*

Inness, and the Art of Painting Softly (Williamstown, Mass.: Sterling and Francine Clark Art Institute, 2008).

37. Leo G. Mazow, "George Inness, Henry George, the Single Tax, and the Future Poet," *American Art* 18 (Spring 2004): 58–77; Inness's comments at the Henry George dinner are quoted in full on p. 75. See Henry George, *Progress and Poverty: An Inquiry into the Cause of Industrial Depressions, and of Increase of Want with Increase of Wealth* (1879; New York: D. Appleton and Company, 1880).

38. Inness, quoted in Inness Jr., *Life, Art, and Letters of George Inness*, 161–62.

39. See Mazow, "George Inness," 65–70; George, *Progress and Poverty*, 7. The figural emphasis is also indebted to the newly formed Society of American Artists, which advocated the human figure as a means of demonstrating artistic accomplishment.

40. On Inness during the Civil War, see Mazow, "George Inness: Problems in Antimodernism" (PhD diss., University of North Carolina at Chapel Hill, 1996), 61–63.

41. R. B. Rosenburg, "Southern Poor Boys" (1993), in Larry M. Logue and Michael Barton, eds., *The Civil War Veteran: A Historical Reader* (New York: New York University Press, 2007), 97.

42. Michael Quick notes the affinities between *In the Gloaming* and the even more recent beggar pictures by Jules Bastien-Lapage in *George Inness: A Catalogue Raisonné*, 2 vols. (New Brunswick, N.J.: Rutgers University Press, 2007), 2:70.

43. Ibid.

44. See Edith Abbott, "The Civil War and the Crime Wave" (1927), in Logue and Barton, eds., *The Civil War Veteran*, 65–79.

45. Eric T. Dean Jr., "Post-Traumatic Stress" (1997), in Logue and Barton, eds., *The Civil War Veteran*, 126–45.

46. "Take-Up Rates for Civil War Pensions," in Theda Skocpol, "America's First Social Security System" (1993), in Logue and Barton, eds., *The Civil War Veteran*, 185, table 13.1.

47. Larry M. Logue, *To Appomattox and Beyond: The Civil War Soldier in War and Peace* (Chicago: Ivan R. Dee, 1996), 89; Michael F. Fitzpatrick, "Payback for Broken Soldiers," *Civil War Times Illustrated* 401, no. 6 (2002): 38–45. Perusing the corpus of veteran pictures, we might keep in mind that, as Logue writes, "Even though veterans' advocates tried to differentiate ex-soldiers from inmates of poorhouses, they could not help viewing veterans as akin to other nineteenth-century dependent groups who were generally believed to be suffering from the moral weakness that could be cured by instilling self-discipline" (p. 92).

48. *Catalogue of the Private Art Collection of Thomas B. Clarke, New York* (New York: American Art Association, 1899), no. 265.

49. T. J. Clark, *The Absolute Bourgeois: Artists and Politics in France, 1848–1851* (Greenwich, Conn.: New York Graphic Society, 1973), 96.

50. Laura L. Meixner, *French Realist Painting and the Critique of American Society, 1865–1900* (New York: Cambridge University Press, 1995).

51. For Inness on Millet, see George W. Sheldon, "Characteristics of George Inness," *The Century* 49, n.s. 27 (February 1895): 533.

52. See Jackson Lears, *No Place of Grace: Antimodernism and the Transformation of American Culture, 1880–1920* (New York: Pantheon, 1981), 142–81.

53. Anna George de Mille, *Henry George: Citizen of the World*, ed. Don C. Shoemaker (Chapel Hill: University of North Carolina Press, 1950), 187; "The George Dinner," *The Standard*, January 22, 1890, pp. 8–11; Daniel Carter Beard, *Hardly a Man is Now Alive: The Autobiography of Dan Beard* (New York: Doubleday, Doran and Company, 1939), 331–32.

54. Kim Moreland, *The Medievalist Impulse in American Literature: Twain, Adams, Fitzgerald, and Hemingway* (Charlottesville: University Press of Virginia, 1996), 49.

55. Our knowledge of Twain's work in these early years is in fact drawn in part from Mills's reminiscences. See, for example, Mills's comments in Victor Fischer and Michael

B. Frank, eds., *Mark Twain's Letters*, 6 vols. (Berkeley: University of California Press, 1992), 3:296n2. See also 3:360n2, where Twain expresses his dissatisfaction with Mills's inability to produce illustrations for his *Buffalo Express* article "The Last Words of Great Men." Mills's autobiography is reprinted in Robert Taft, *Artists and Illustrators of the Old West: 1850–1900* (Princeton: Princeton University Press, 1982), 345–47.

56. Twain, "Salutatory," *Buffalo Express*, August 21, 1869; reprinted in Joseph B. McCullough and Janice McIntire-Strasburg, eds., *Mark Twain at the* Buffalo Express: *Articles and Sketches by America's Favorite Humorist* (DeKalb: Northern Illinois University Press, 1999), 6.

57. By 1865, the government had imposed a 5 percent tax on incomes between $600 and $5,000 and a 10 percent tax on incomes over $5,000. See William L. Barney, *Battleground for the Union: The Era of the Civil War and Reconstruction, 1848–1877* (Englewood Cliffs, N.J.: Prentice Hall, 1990), 164; and W. Elliot Brownlee, *Federal Taxation in America: A Short History* (Washington, D.C.: Woodrow Wilson Center Press; Cambridge: Cambridge University Press, 1996), 26–28.

58. I first presented the material on Mills and Twain in an object entry in Joyce Henri Robinson's catalogue *An Endless Panorama of Beauty: Selections from the Jean and Alvin Snowiss Collection of American Art* (University Park: Palmer Museum of Art, The Pennsylvania State University, 2002), 79.

59. Mrs. Burton Harrison, "Wanted: A Chaperon," ill. Henry Hutt, *Saturday Evening Post*, April 15, 1899, pp. 657–58; Harrison, *The Carcellini, with Other Tales* (New York: Herbert S. Stone and Company, 1899), following p. 288. On Hutt, see Rowland Elzea and Iris Snyder, *The American Illustration Collections of the Delaware Art Museum* (Wilmington: Delaware Art Museum, 1991), 185.

60. Harrison, "Wanted: A Chaperon," pp. 657, 658.

61. Jackson Lears, *Rebirth of a Nation: The Making of Modern America, 1877–1920* (New York: Harper, 2009), 67.

62. Harrison, "Wanted: A Chaperon," pp. 657, 658.

63. Lears, *Rebirth of a Nation*, 93.

64. See http://www.themorris.org/ourcollection/morrison-weighing.html.

65. *Catalogue of the Private Art Collection of Thomas B. Clarke*, 75; no. 90. Clarke's catalogue gives the dimensions of *Rent Day* as 32 × 43 inches. The painted version of *Rent Day* indeed features a rent agent, there to collect his money, at far left; reproduced in H. Barbara Weinberg, "Thomas B. Clarke: Foremost Patron of American Art from 1872 to 1889," *American Art Journal* 8 (May 1976): 81.

66. Joseph Boskin, *Sambo: The Rise and Demise of an American Jester* (New York: Oxford University Press, 1986); Jo-Ann Morgan, "Selling the Old South for the New Century," *American Art* 9, no. 1 (1995): 86–109; Elizabeth L. O'Leary, *At Beck and Call: The Representation of Domestic Servants in Nineteenth-Century American Painting* (Washington, D.C.: Smithsonian Institution Press, 1996), 132, 144–45.

67. Stowe, quoted in O'Leary, *At Beck and Call*, 145.

68. Eric Foner, *Reconstruction: America's Unfinished Revolution, 1863–1877* (New York: Harper and Row, 1988), 429.

69. On the "headwrap as a distinct badge of black servility," see O'Leary, *At Beck and Call*, 146.

70. "Laying in Rum for Sunday," *Harper's Weekly* 11, February 16, 1868, p. 1.

71. The artist has confirmed the national identity of the yellow-clad woman (taken from a nineteenth-century Brazilian lithograph) as well as the Marx reference; Maya Fineberg, e-mail correspondence with author, December 16, 2009.

72. T. S. Eliot, "Burnt Norton," lines 42–43, in Eliot, *Four Quartets* (1943; reprint, New York: Harcourt Books, 1971), 14.

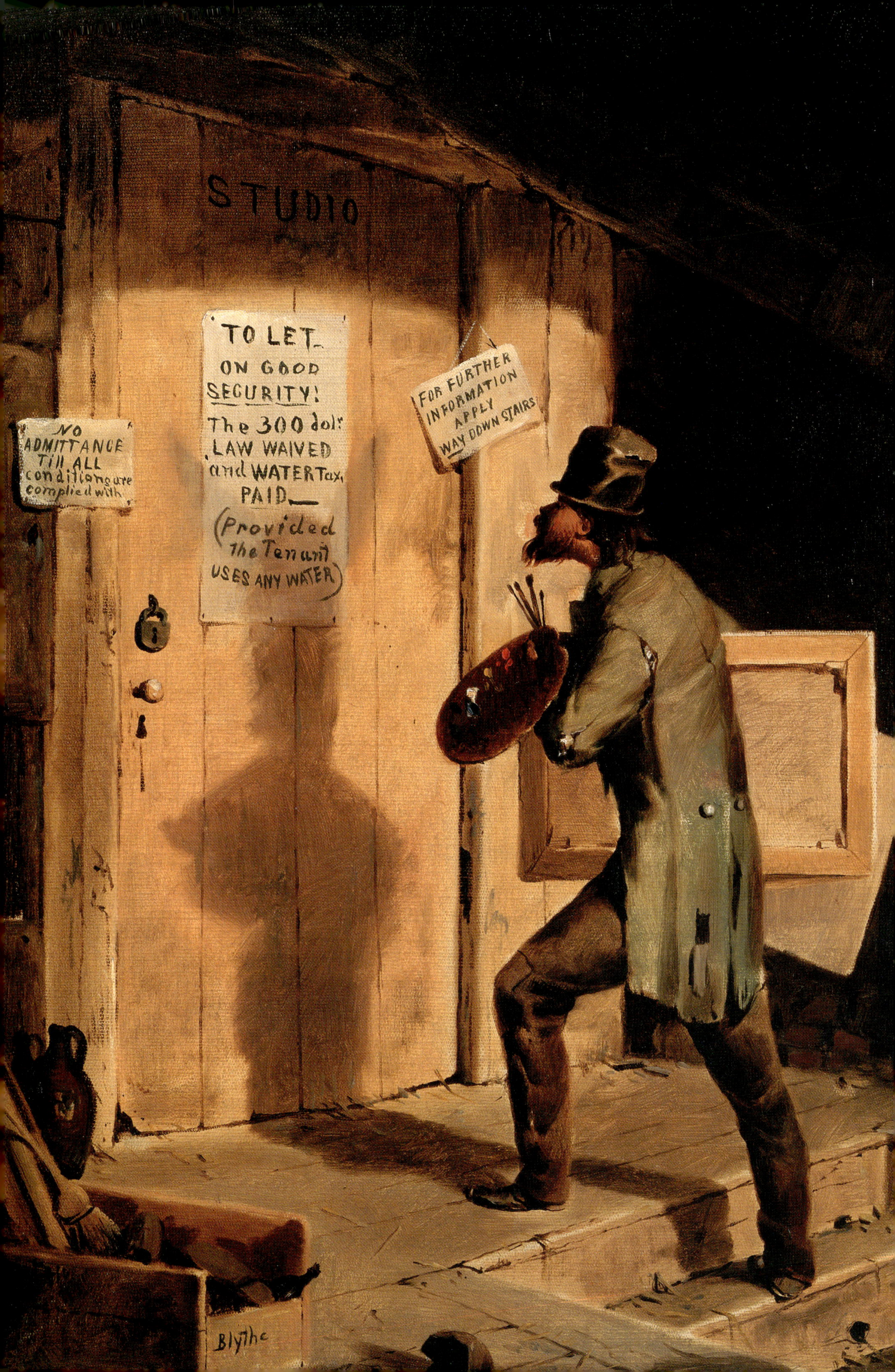
STUDIO
TO LET
ON GOOD
SECURITY!
The 300 dol:
LAW WAIVED
and WATER Tax
PAID
(Provided
the Tenant
USES ANY WATER)
NO
ADMITTANCE
Till ALL
conditions are
complied with
FOR FURTHER
INFORMATION
APPLY
WAY DOWN STAIRS
Blythe

The Poor Artist?
American Art in an Era of Financial Panic, Depression, and Speculation

KEVIN M. MURPHY

On the eve of the Civil War, genre painter David Gilmour Blythe created *Art Versus Law* (1859–60), depicting an artist who has been evicted and locked out of his run-down attic studio, presumably for his inability to pay rent (fig. 32). The unfortunate artist in the work has always been considered a self-portrait of Blythe, and the painting's first owner believed that it represented an incident from the artist's life.[1] A few years later, the painter James Beard produced a remarkably similar scene in *Studio to Let* (1864; fig. 33). The consequences for Blythe's and Beard's artists are particularly dire, as eviction from the studio deprived them of the means of not only producing but also selling their work, since the studio often doubled as a showroom. Rent is also a concern in John Harrison Mills's *Artist Painting a Satirical Painting* (1870s–80s; fig. 34). In a bare studio, furnished with a chair, stove, and easel, an artist entertains a comely visitor by updating a medieval battle scene. In the center of the painting, a red-cloaked knight combats three foes that the artist has labeled "taxes," "bills," and "rent." But of the three only rent, who lies on the ground, has been vanquished; whether the knight will conquer the evils of taxes and bills remains to be seen.[2] In the lower right-hand corner of the painting, the artist has written "Class 2/No Bids," suggesting that the work may have come back unsold from a venue such as the National Academy of Design in New York, prompting him to deface the apparently valueless painting.[3]

In the 1880s, Albert Pinkham Ryder commented on the paltry financial and social rewards for American painters in *The Poor Artist* (n.d.; fig. 35). The titular figure, who resembles photographs and portraits of Ryder,[4] shuffles down a city street with his head bowed, carrying a small canvas or portfolio under his right arm. As art historian William Innes Homer noted, Ryder isolated the artist spatially by placing him in the center of the composition, separated from the two girls on the left as well as the mother and child at right. Members of the flanking groups interact with one another but ignore the artist, and all four figures look and move in the opposite direction to him, suggesting his social alienation.[5] The two girls on the left peer covetously at goods displayed in the shop window, in a gesture of desire similar

Opposite
Detail of figure 32.

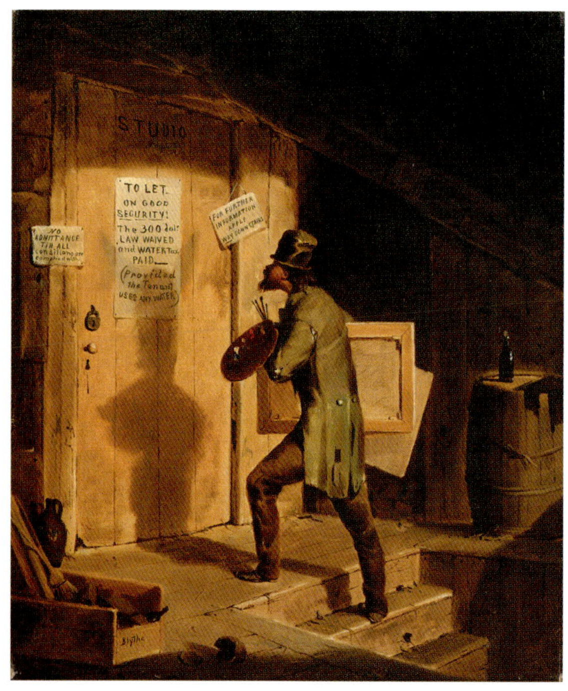

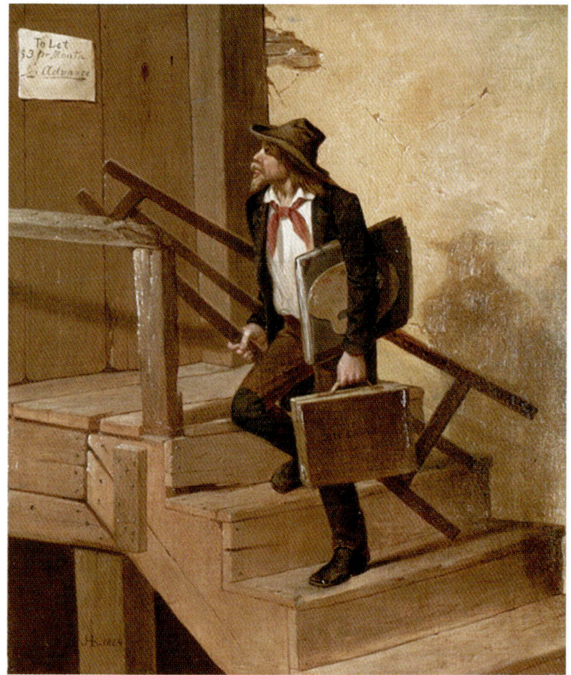

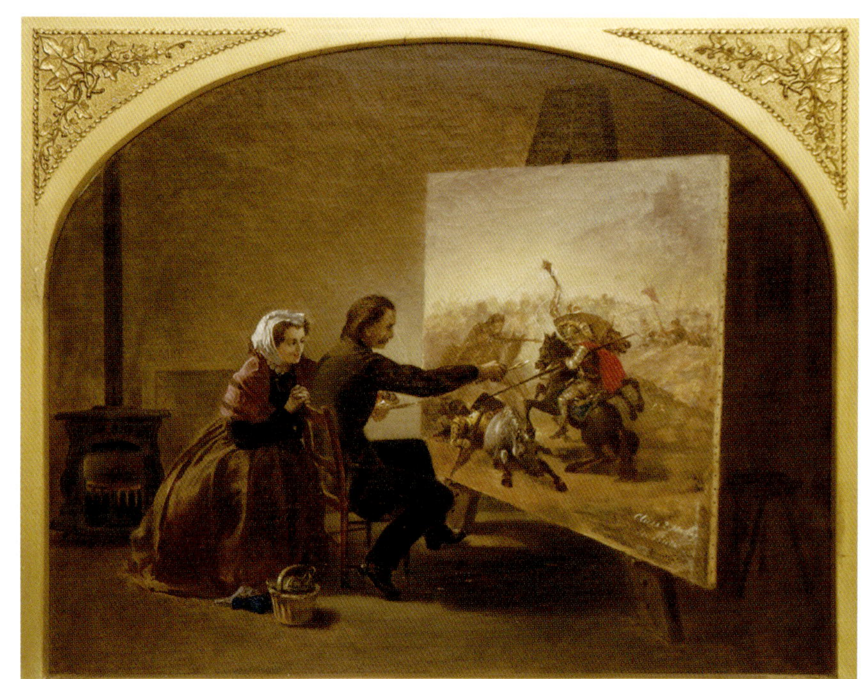

Figure 32
David Gilmour Blythe, *Art Versus Law*, 1859–60, oil on canvas, 24 x 35 13/16 inches. Brooklyn Museum. Dick S. Ramsay Fund, 40.907.
IN EXHIBITION

Figure 33
James Henry Beard, *Studio to Let*, 1864, oil on canvas, 16 5/8 x 13 3/4 inches. Herbert F. Johnson Museum of Art, Cornell University. Acquired through the Ernest I. White, Class of 1893, Endowment Fund. Photograph courtesy of the Herbert F. Johnson Museum of Art, Cornell University.
IN EXHIBITION

Figure 34
John Harrison Mills, *Artist Painting a Satirical Painting*, ca. 1870s–80s, oil on canvas, 20 x 24½ inches. Collection of Jean and Alvin Snowiss.
IN EXHIBITION

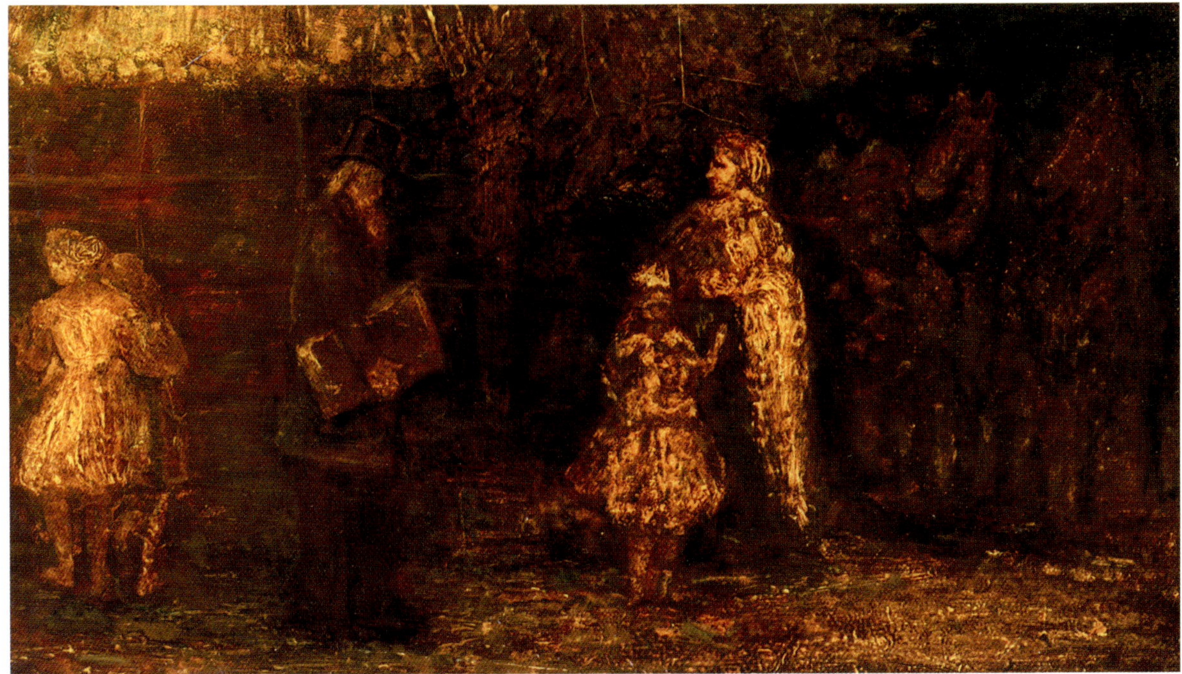

Figure 35
Albert Pinkham Ryder, *The Poor Artist*, n.d., oil on canvas, 7 ⁷⁄₁₆ x 12 inches. Princeton University Art Museum. Gift of Alastair B. Martin, Class of 1938, y1957-11. Photo: Bruce M. White.
IN EXHIBITION

to that found in James Whistler's *A Chelsea Shop* (ca. 1894–95), but remain oblivious to the artist and his wares, suggesting Ryder's isolation from the realm of commerce as well (fig. 36). Contemporary accounts confirm that Ryder's work had all but no market. *New York Times* art critic Charles de Kay wrote in 1890: "Ryder has little financial fame. Art dealers for the most part shrug their shoulders over his pictures. The regular buyers at the sales would much sooner 'handle' . . . the worst daub by a modern Italian and in horrible taste than one of Mr. Ryder's little jewels."[6]

In this brief passage, de Kay touched on three problems that many American artists believed were detrimental to their livelihood—the attitudes of art dealers, the system of auction sales, and the preference for foreign art. The sale of artworks through dealers and at auctions marked a major shift. Up to this time, artists had sold work through traditional forms of patronage, visits by collectors to their studios, and professional organizations such as the National Academy of Design. Now artists were convinced that the more consumer-oriented venues of commercial galleries, exhibitions, and auctions diverted profits into the hands of middlemen and speculators. Landscape painter Jervis McEntee, who kept a detailed diary from 1872 to 1890, believed that dealers and critics conspired against American artists: "[T]he dealers who carefully form the popular judgment have no sympathy for us. The Press finds it profitable to keep in the good graces of the dealers, so that it is actually the case now that there is no place in New York where the leading American Artists can send their pictures for sale with the hope of

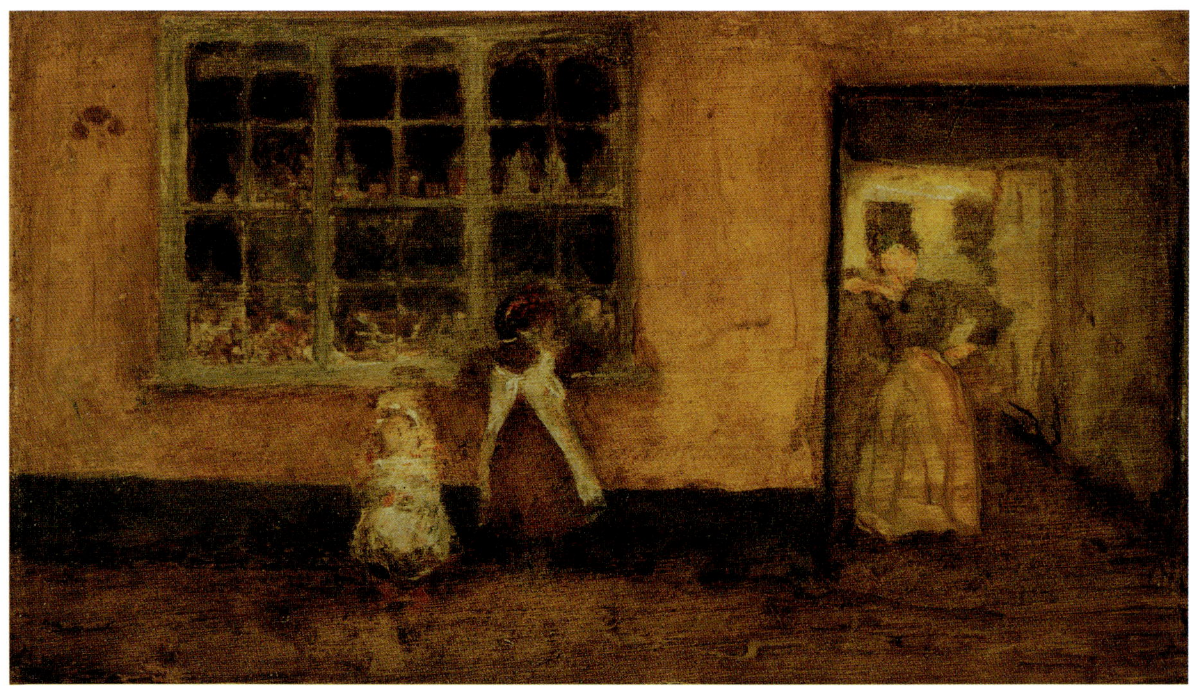

Figure 36
James McNeill Whistler, *A Chelsea Shop*, 1894–95, oil on panel, 5 x 8 7/16 inches. Terra Foundation for American Art, Chicago, Daniel J. Terra Collection, 1992.148. Photo: Terra Foundation for American Art, Chicago / Art Resource, NY.
IN EXHIBITION

Figure 37 (opposite)
Julian Alden Weir, *The Flower Seller*, ca. 1879, oil on canvas, 40 3/8 x 22 1/8 inches. Brooklyn Museum. Gift of George A. Hearn, 11.522.
IN EXHIBITION

finding anything like fair treatment."[7] The quantity of foreign art for sale in the United States increased—in large part due to the efforts of art dealers—after the Civil War, further squeezing the market share of American art.[8] In 1874, the painter Worthington Whittredge (see fig. 48) complained that "immense numbers of pictures . . . are imported and seem to find sale, some at enormous prices, while the [Albert] Bierstadts, and [Frederic] Churches, [Sanford] Giffords and [Eastman] Johnsons are not sold or even wanted. Some better disposition must be shown for at least our good artists or art here and our art institutions must die out. It has become I think a little too much the custom to depreciate everything produced here and over[-]estimate everything brought from abroad."[9] Whittredge's prediction epitomizes the dark mood of some American artists as they contemplated their economic prospects, particularly in relation to foreign competition.

Macroeconomic factors also contributed to the unfavorable market for luxury goods such as paintings; the era saw several "panics" that disrupted commerce and decimated wealth, two severe depressions—from 1873 to 1877 and 1893 to 1897—as well as significant deflation, which put downward pressure on prices and wages, including the prices for artwork. It was at the beginning of the depression of the 1870s, in 1874, when Whittredge expressed his fear that American art would "die out" for the lack of a market. Some twenty years later, during the next depression, the most acute up to that time, portrait painter J. Carroll Beckwith wished that "someone would come and give me some work. I would paint portraits for $10 apiece gladly if I could get the sitters and dared come down on my price. Which by the way is wildly absurd when one thinks of the microscopic demand." In June 1895, he lamented, "It is needless to say I have no balance left at the bank."[10]

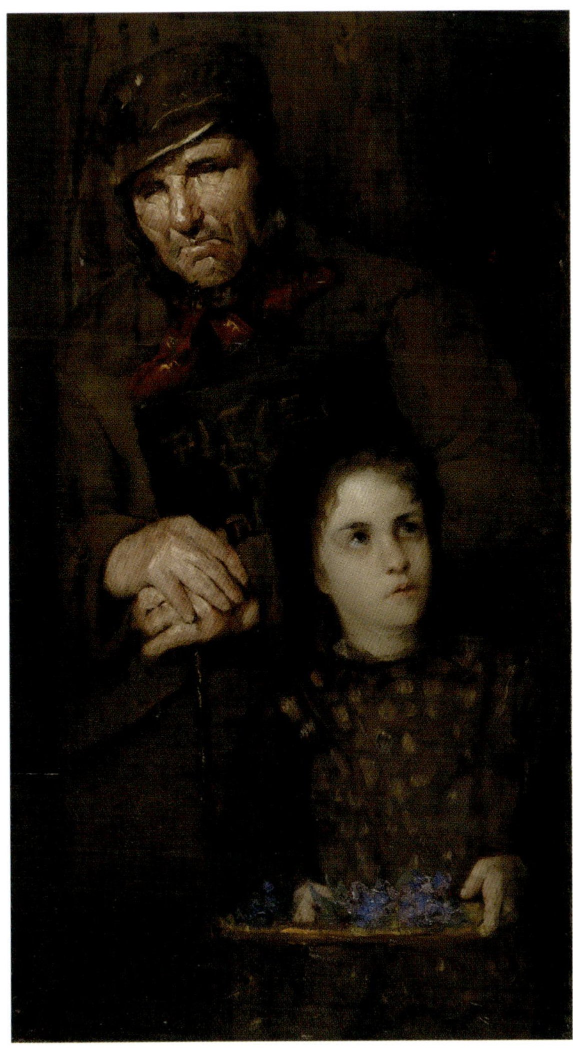

Facing these conditions, it is little wonder that Blythe, Beard, and Ryder painted themselves as just a step removed from the indigent woman in Alfred Kappes's *Tattered and Torn* (1886) and J. Alden Weir's blind beggar in *The Flower Seller* (ca. 1879) (figs. 28, 37). Artists understood their precarious place in the American economy all too well, feeling very much at the mercy of Adam Smith's invisible hand. These fears, as well as severe hardships in the country as a whole, may have made artists sympathetic to the downtrodden. Although desperate for money, J. Carroll Beckwith nonetheless wrote in his diary about those less fortunate than himself—two of his models—and hoped for a remedy to the conditions that fostered inequality in wealth: "Heavens! When I think that we paid $18 for our dinner last night . . . and here are two girls who have been in my studio today who are absolutely penniless. It makes me ill. There is something radically wrong in things somewhere." Beckwith noted that he paid the women $2 apiece for their modeling, more than his normal rate, between $1 and $1.50.[11]

In addition to painting images of the poor, American artists painted scenes that related specifically to the financial panics of the later nineteenth century and their aftermath. James Cafferty and Charles G. Rosenberg portrayed some of the men involved in the first sudden downturn of the period in *Wall Street, Half Past Two O'Clock, October 13, 1857* (1858; fig. 38). The Panic of 1857, which began with a slowdown in western expansion that made it difficult for many businesses, particularly banks and railroads, to meet their financial obligations, culminated on October 13 when banks throughout the country suspended operations and effectively shut down the economy.[12] Cafferty and Rosenberg, in turn, depicted Wall Street traders and tycoons, including Cornelius Vanderbilt on the far right of the painting, who have left the trading floors and poured into the street.[13]

In view of the chaos of the plummeting markets and lost fortunes, the relatively calm demeanor of the stockbrokers in Cafferty and Rosenberg's

Figure 38
James Henry Cafferty and Charles G. Rosenberg, *Wall Street, Half Past Two O'Clock, October 13, 1857*, 1858, oil on canvas, 50 x 40 inches. Museum of the City of New York. Gift of the Honorable Irwin Untermeyer, 40.54.
IN EXHIBITION

Figure 39 (opposite)
Cafferty, *The Weary Newsboy*, 1861, detail of fig. 6.
IN EXHIBITION

Figure 40 (opposite)
David Gilmour Blythe, *A Match Seller*, ca. 1859, oil on canvas, 27 x 22 inches. North Carolina Museum of Art. Purchased with funds from the State of North Carolina.
IN EXHIBITION

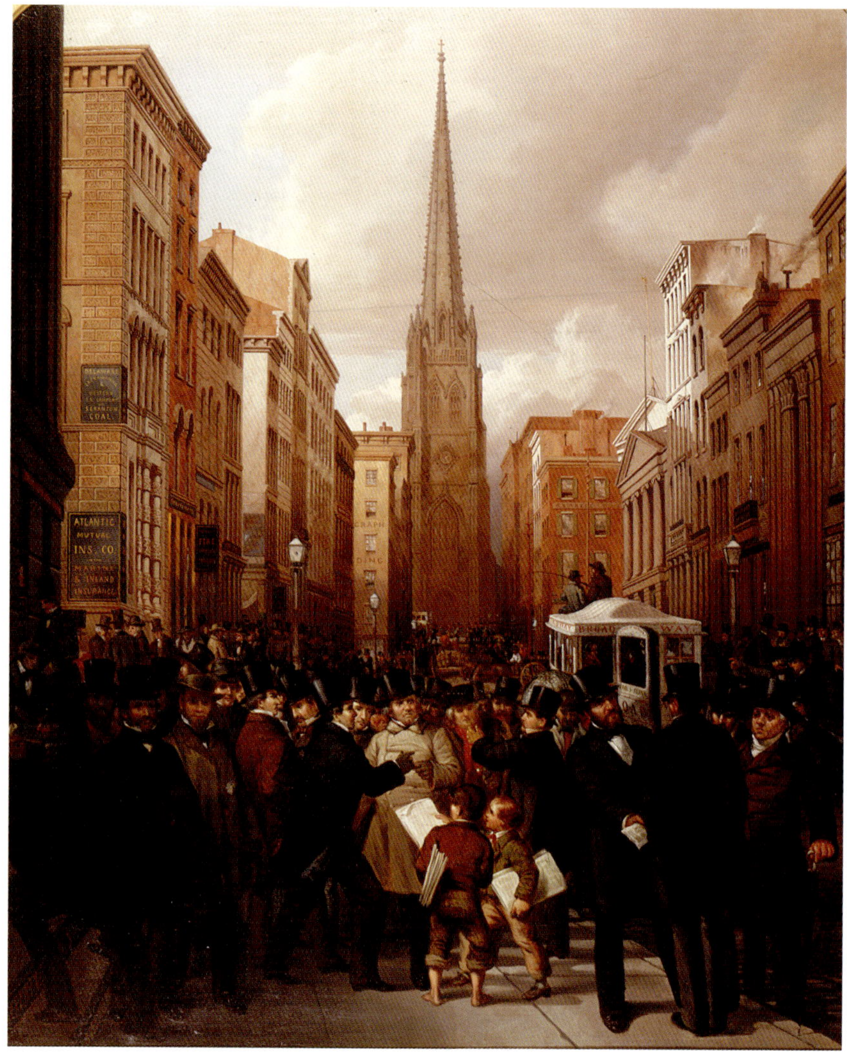

depiction may have evoked a contrast in the minds of New Yorkers between the businessmen and unruly lower-class immigrant gangs that fought protracted street battles in 1857. Cafferty and Rosenberg did include two newsboys in the foreground, however. As Leo Mazow notes in his essay in this catalogue, scenes of newsboys, bootblacks, and flower sellers—such as Henry Mosler's *The Fair Exchange* (1881) and John George Brown's *Buy a Posy* (1886) and *A Tough Story* (1886)—portrayed poverty as picturesque rather than squalid (see figs. 7–9), which ensured the popularity of such paintings despite their depiction of systemic inequities in American society. I would also argue that the entrepreneurial behavior of the newsboys in *Half Past Two*, as well as that of the children in the paintings by Brown and Mosler—but also in earlier, less cheerful pieces such as Cafferty's *Weary Newsboy* (1861) and Blythe's *Match Seller* (ca. 1859)—helps mitigate their status as members of the "dangerous classes" (figs. 39, 40). Somewhat paradoxically,

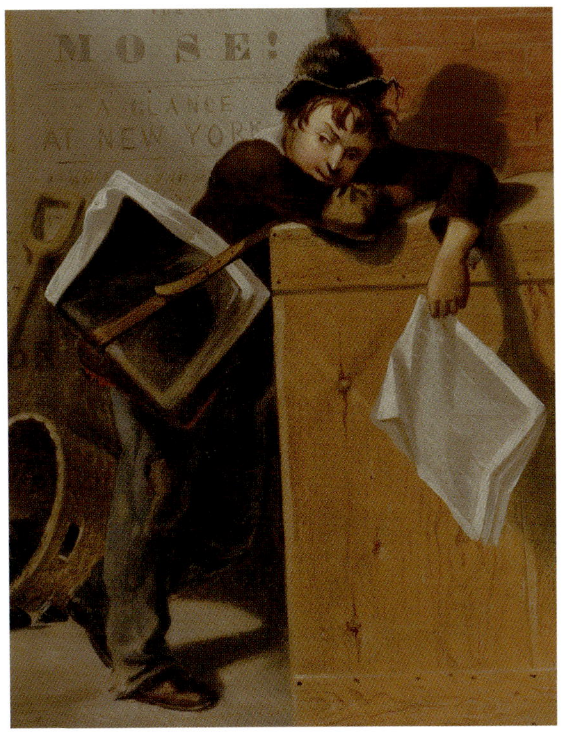

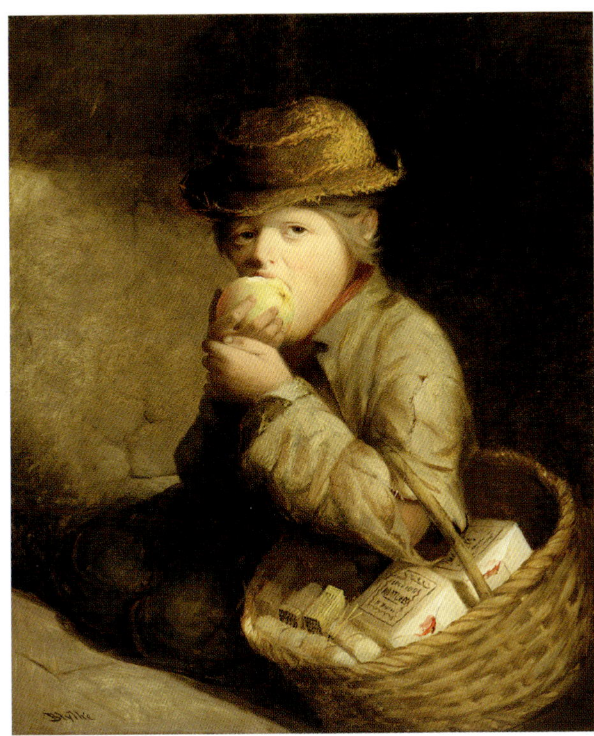

their engagement in trade links them to the bankers and brokers. Although poor, the children are engaging in commerce on a small scale, striving to surmount their material hardships.

By contrast, Indiana-based painter Ellen Ingraham's *Out of Work* (n.d.) raised the disturbing possibility that there could be a permanent class of paupers dependent on public and private charity, ending any pretense that America's great natural resources and democratic government would allow everyone to become self-sufficient merchants, farmers, or artisans (fig. 41).[14] During each of the depressions in the nineteenth century, debates arose regarding the treatment of those rendered poor by economic circumstances beyond their control. In the aftermath of the Panic of 1857, for example, the New York Association for Improving Conditions of the Poor, of which Cornelius Vanderbilt was a member, called a program "communistic" that was to provide work-relief to the poor by having them help build Central Park.[15] Some members of the upper classes opposed charitable relief in any form because they feared handouts of money, services, and even work-relief would accustom poor people to receiving things for free, thereby eroding their work ethic.[16]

German immigrant Charles Knoll painted an intimate scene of the effects of the Panic of 1869 on a bourgeois family (1869; fig. 42). In the *Panic of 1869*, a man has collapsed in a chair, having just dropped at his feet a newspaper in which he would have read of his catastrophic losses from speculating

Figure 41
Ellen M. Ingraham, *Out of Work*, n.d., oil on canvas, 30 x 24¾ inches. Indianapolis Museum of Art. Gift of Miss Lena L. Ingraham, 23.79.
IN EXHIBITION

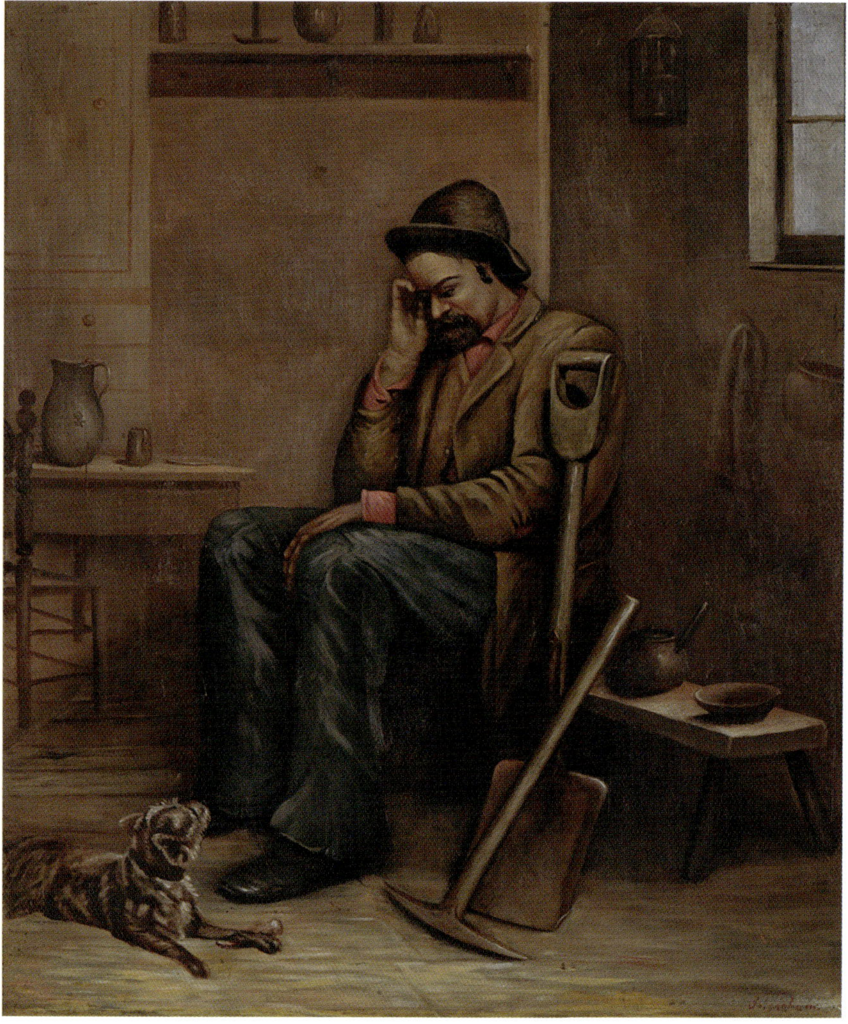

in gold or stocks during Jay Gould's and Jim Fisk's unsuccessful attempt to corner the gold market.[17] Although his wife holds his hand to comfort him, she looks away apprehensively, perhaps considering the likely effect of the news on their standard of living, signified by the home's opulent interior, filled with paintings, prints, mirrors with gilt frames, and furniture upholstered in bright, aniline dyes.

The sympathy and sensitivity shown by Cafferty, Rosenberg, and Knoll to those affected by the myriad and sudden economic downturns of the era may have stemmed in part from artists' own participation in what novelist, historian, and social critic Henry Adams termed the "speculative mania" gripping the country, in which "almost every man who had money employed a part of his capital in the purchase of stocks or of gold, of copper, of petroleum, or of domestic produce, in the hope of a rise in prices, or staked money on the expectation of a fall."[18] Cafferty included himself among the

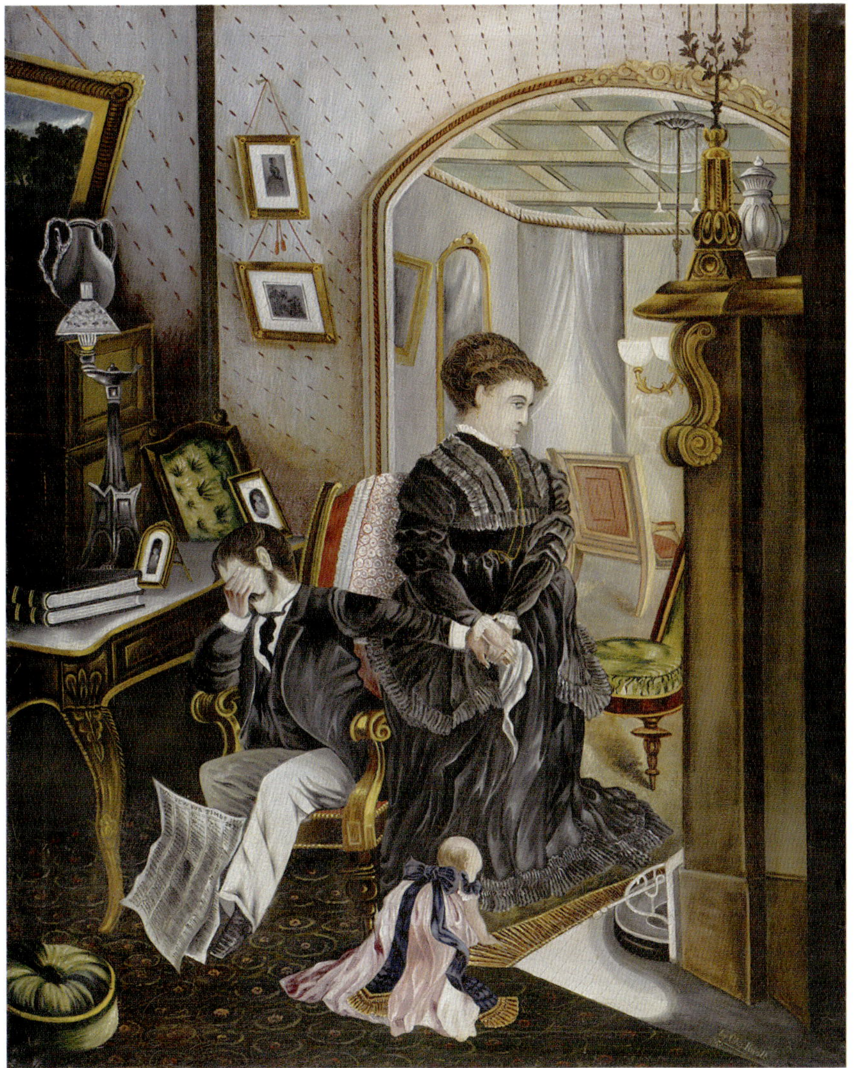

Figure 42
Charles Knoll, *Panic of 1869*, 1869, oil on canvas, 34½ x 27 inches. Colby College Museum of Art, Waterville, Maine. Gift of Mr. and Mrs. Ellerton M. Jetté.
IN EXHIBITION

Wall Street speculators as the bearded figure wearing a light-colored coat on the left side of *Wall Street, Half Past Two O'Clock October 13, 1857*.[19] Winslow Homer speculated heavily in real estate in Prout's Neck, Maine. Portrait painter J. Carroll Beckwith owned stock in railroads and banks, and invested in New York and Chicago real estate.[20] Albert Bierstadt held equities in a variety of enterprises, including the Brown Segmental Tube Wire Gun Company, Sovereign Mining Company, the Anderson Coke, Gas, and Manufacturing Company, and the Telautograph Company. However, like the poor fellow in *Panic of 1869*, Bierstadt overextended himself and declared bankruptcy in 1895.[21] Art dealer James Inglis reported that even the reclusive and mystical Albert Pinkham Ryder hatched a scheme in which he would sell enough paintings "to buy himself $4,500 of Pullman stock which would give him an annual income of $350 on which he says he can live,"

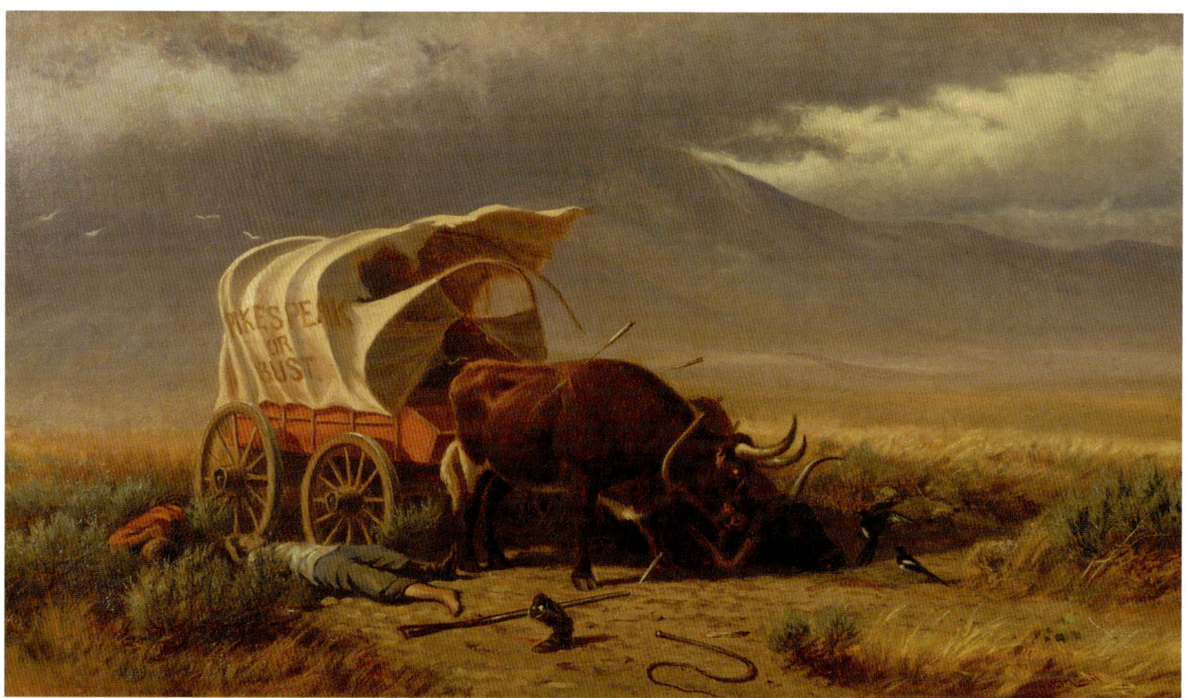

Figure 43
William de la Montaigne Cary, *Pikes Peak's or Bust*, early 1870s, oil on canvas, 21 x 36 inches. Hood Museum of Art, Dartmouth College. Purchased through the Guernsey Center Moore 1904 Memorial Fund.
IN EXHIBITION

Figure 44 (opposite)
Gustave Kruell, after Alfred Kappes, *Rent Day*, detail of fig. 26.

suggesting just how pervasive Adams's "speculative mania" became in the later decades of the nineteenth century.[22] The consequences of speculation in gold is also the subject of William de la Montagne Cary's *Pike's Peak or Bust* (early 1870s), although here the stakes are not simply the loss of material comforts and bourgeois prerogatives, but life itself (fig. 43). The slogan "Pike's Peak or Bust" referred to the Colorado Gold Rush that began at the end of the 1850s. Cary's would-be prospector, however, will never make it to the gold fields beyond the Rocky Mountains.

The jargon of Wall Street found its way into the language of artists, dealers, and critics. In 1882, Winslow Homer (see fig. 45) indicated to Boston art dealer J. Eastman Chase that he intended to "make a 'corner' on my work"—that is, to have strict control over the supply of his paintings on the market so that he could better control their prices, as speculators did by buying up a majority of shares in a company or of a commodity.[23] Homer also used such language in a letter to art dealers M. Knoedler and Company, regarding the difficulty he had pricing his paintings: "I do not know the price of January pictures. You must keep me informed that I may be long or short on them as the market fluctuates."[24] James Inglis suggested to collector Charles Erskine Scott Wood that they form a "Syndicate" to buy work by French artist Adolphe Monticelli in 1897.[25] Artists' participation in speculative activity did not pass without comment. Clarence Cook, outspoken critic for the New York *Tribune*, inveighed, "there is as much speculation, as much strategy, and as much trickery employed to-day by certain artists in selling their pictures as there is among certain Wall Street men in selling

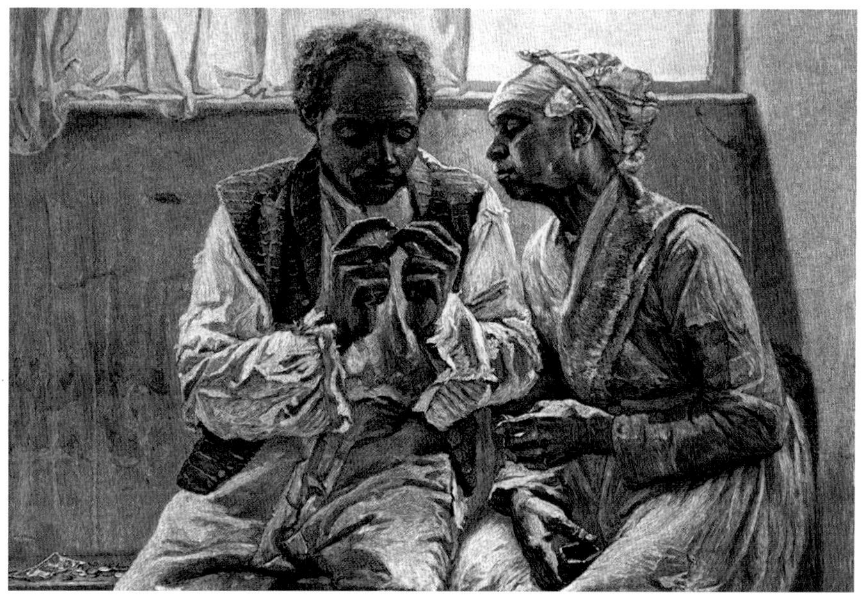

stocks; and the mercantile, trading spirit . . . threatens to retard the growth of a genuine art in this country, if not kill it altogether."[26] Painter Worthington Whittredge believed that American art would "die out" because of a lack of market, while the critic Cook felt American art to be doomed because artists were too forceful in their commercial ambitions: the gulf between these views reveals something about the artist's struggle to survive economically during the nineteenth century, in a cultural milieu that increasingly saw art as sacred, above the fray of mercantile exchange.

Artists were themselves ambivalent about commercial engagement: they may have been willing to speculate in stocks and real estate, and sometimes applied strategies of stock manipulation to the selling of their own work, but they resented the entry of speculators into the market. Homer did not want Roland Knoedler to sell one of his paintings to a client that the artist considered "a speculator—he wishes a share in this picture and still leaving it in your hands—thinking to make a dollar or two . . . I have met these people before and be D=== to them."[27] One such speculator was dry goods merchant Thomas B. Clarke, who amassed a large collection of American art between 1872 and 1899 and then auctioned off all of it. Although some viewed the solid prices at the Clarke sale as a positive sign of the marketability of American art, others saw Clarke chiefly as taking advantage of American artists.[28] James Inglis judged him "no patron of Art...but a selfish pig."[29] Clarke owned Alfred Kappes' s *Rent Day*, after which Gustave Kruell produced a wood engraving (1887), as well as Eastman Johnson's *The Pension Claim Agent* (1867) (figs. 44, 19).[30] He purchased Johnson's painting at the 1891 auction of another "incurable speculator in pictures," banker George Seney.[31]

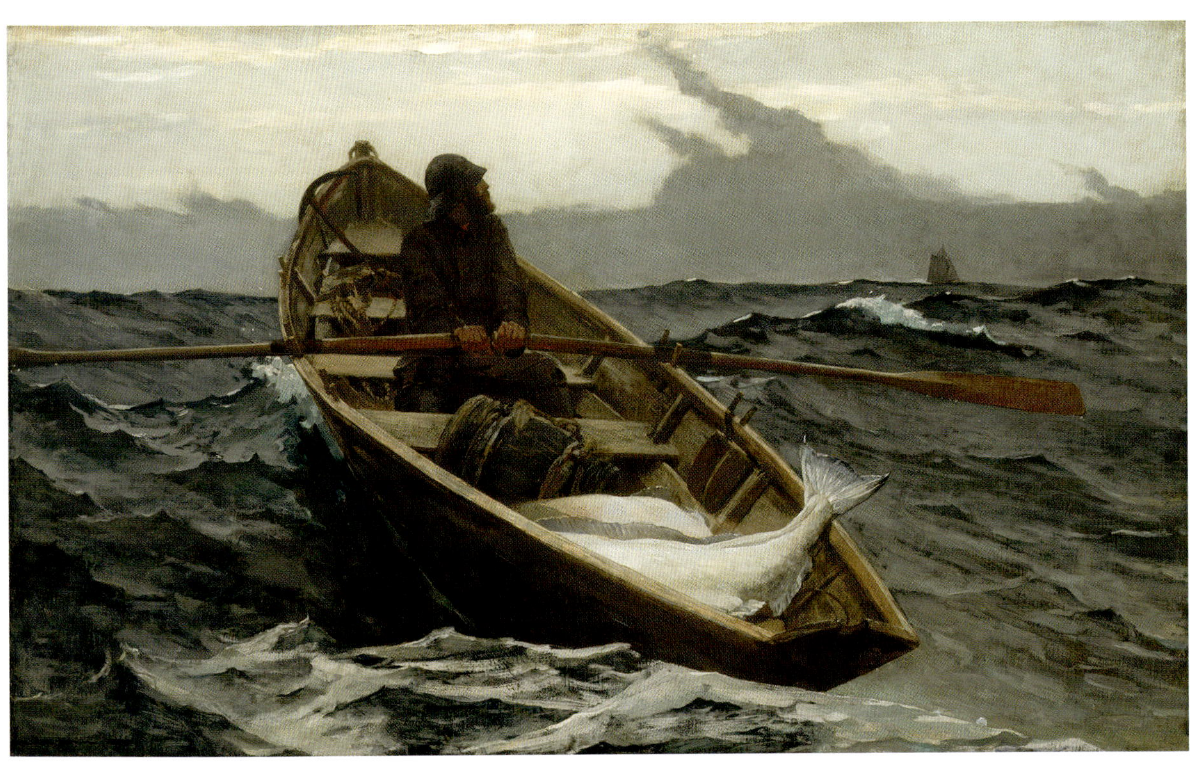

Figure 45
Winslow Homer, *The Fog Warning*, 1885, oil on canvas, 30¼ x 48½ inches. Museum of Fine Arts, Boston. Otis Norcross Fund, 94.72.

Speculators profited from the products of the artist's intellectual and physical labor—without any additional reward coming back to the artist. In their opposition to this arrangement, artists participated in a larger societal debate about the rights of workers versus the rentier class, during an era in which disparity between haves and have-nots grew ever wider, as well as particular disputes over the ownership of art.[32] Inglis had been extremely annoyed at Clarke because he sawed in half a wood panel Ryder painted on both sides, and sold each painting separately, in essence getting a free Ryder painting.[33] Ryder himself believed that artists maintained rights over their production even after a "sale," invoking James Whistler: "I refer you to the verdict of the English court justifying Whistler's contention that a man did not wholly own a painting by simply buying it."[34] Ryder's friend and patron, Charles Wood, an occasional art dealer, admitted to J. Alden Weir: "It is not a fair division between the creator of a work of art and the mere dealer."[35] As noted elsewhere in this catalogue, George Inness accused the owner of one of his landscapes of theft when she did not reveal that she had found the *Old Veteran* (ca. 1881) hidden underneath the original canvas (see fig. 16). Inness's assertion of his rights as a producer is congruent with his support for Henry George's Single Tax, which he hoped could help return America to an idyllic, egalitarian society of farmers and craftspeople, of the kind valorized in Homer's *The Fog Warning* (1885; fig. 45) and *The Veteran in a New Field* (1865; Metropolitan Museum of Art).[36]

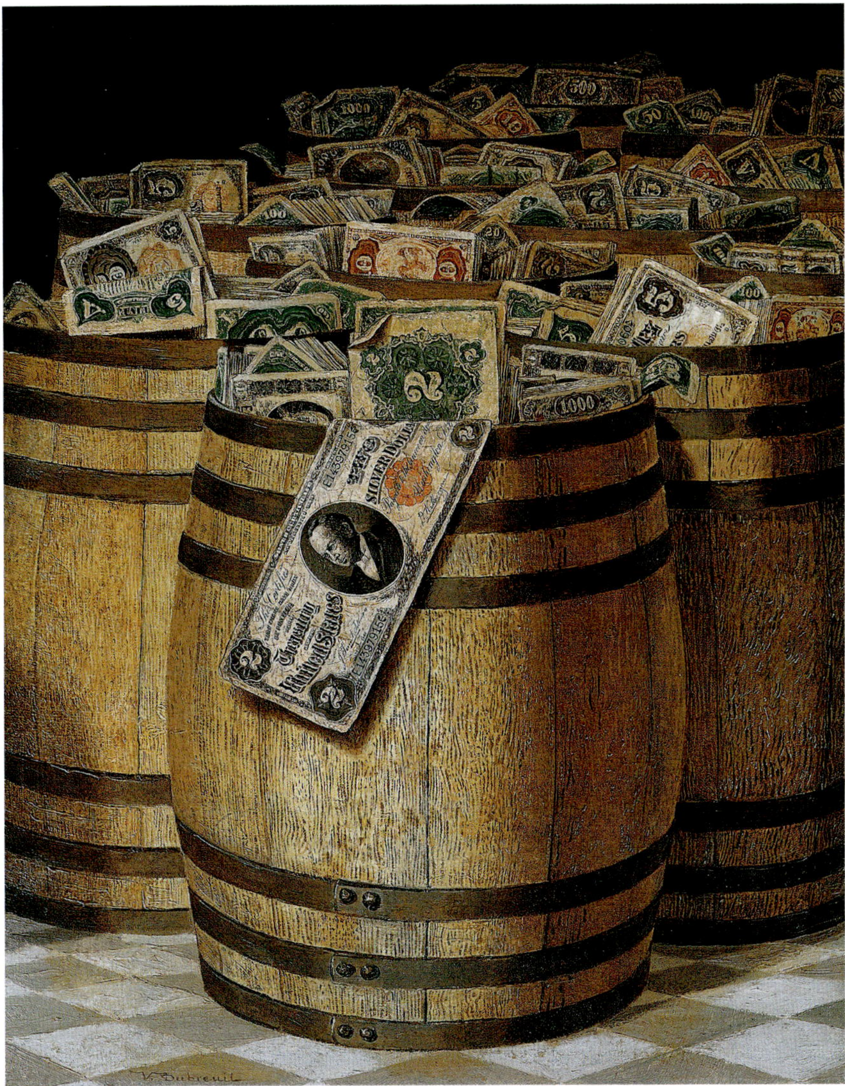

Figure 46
Victor Dubreuil, *Barrels of Money*, ca. 1898, oil on canvas, 24 x 18 inches. Private collection. Courtesy of Berry-Hill Galleries, New York.

Evidence of artists' engagement in the larger economic issues of the day is also found in a remarkable group of trompe l'oeil still-life paintings featuring precisely rendered currency created by several artists, including the best-known trompe l'oeil painters of the era, William Harnett and John Peto. Victor Dubreuil produced two of the most evocative and engaging examples in *Barrels of Money* (ca. 1898) and *Cross of Gold* (ca. 1896). *Barrels of Money* features a dazzling array of banknotes, from two-dollar silver certificates with a portrait of Treasury Secretary William Windom to thousand-dollar bills featuring Civil War General Gordon Meade, and many denominations in between (fig. 46). As art historians Edward Nygren and Bruce Chambers have shown, images such as *Barrels of Money* demonstrate America's cultural fascination with wealth and money during the Gilded Age, but also raise issues of income inequality.[37] The barrels are arranged on a tile floor, as if "extending to infinity," as Chambers put it, suggesting that they are locked

Figure 47
Victor Dubreuil, *The Cross of Gold*, ca. 1896, oil on canvas, 14 x 12 inches. Private collection. Courtesy of Berry-Hill Galleries, New York.
IN EXHIBITION

in the vault of a grand mansion. Such an immense trove of cash may have connoted the activities of men such as Cornelius Vanderbilt and John D. Rockefeller, who attempted to suppress competition in their industries by forming monopolistic trusts, quite literally hoarding the means of producing, transporting, and selling goods and services.[38] The trompe l'oeil paintings of money may also have been provocative to their nineteenth-century viewers, particularly during the deep economic depression of the 1890s. So realistic that they were confiscated by Treasury agents as counterfeit money, the currency paintings by Dubreuil and Harnett are, of course, meticulously rendered fictions.[39]

The sheer quantity of notes in *Barrels of Money*, stockpiled in a vault and backed by different types of specie—silver and gold—alluded to problems in America's money supply in the late nineteenth century. The Panic of 1857 was exacerbated to a large degree by shortages in the amount of gold needed for the economy to function. To finance the Civil War, the United States issued a fiat currency, called "greenbacks" because of the color of the ink used on them. The presence of greenbacks was inflationary, because it increased the amount of money available. After the war, however, the government began removing greenbacks from circulation to bring the value of the notes up to par with gold, eventually resuming the gold standard in 1879.[40] Contraction of the money supply led to falling prices and higher interest, which hurt farmers in the west and south disproportionately; industrialists and their wage-earning employees in the northeast fared better. Loans made to farmers for land and technology while money was relatively cheap and plentiful in the 1860s and early 1870s became difficult to pay back with scarcer dollars. In addition, the downward trend in prices meant farmers received less for their crops, leading to massive indebtedness, the crop lien system, and sharecropping. Conditions in the south were particularly grim, as depicted in Hal Alexander Courtney Morrison's *Weighing the Cotton* (1885–90; fig. 48).[41] To alleviate the currency crisis, many farmers, artisans, and manual laborers living in the west and south urged the government to increase the amount of money in circulation, either by continuing to issue greenbacks or by authorizing the free coinage of silver, while northeastern industrialists generally favored the resumption of the gold standard.[42]

Dubreuil addressed the climax of nineteenth-century America's debates over monetary policy in *Cross of Gold*, an image of currency pinned by four brass nails to a vertical surface in a cruciform shape (fig. 47). The painting refers to the famous campaign speech given by presidential candidate William Jennings Bryan at the Democratic convention in Chicago on July 9, 1896. Bryan ran on a platform that promised the free coinage of silver to solve the financial problems of the west and south, in opposition to the Republican candidate William McKinley's support for the gold stan-

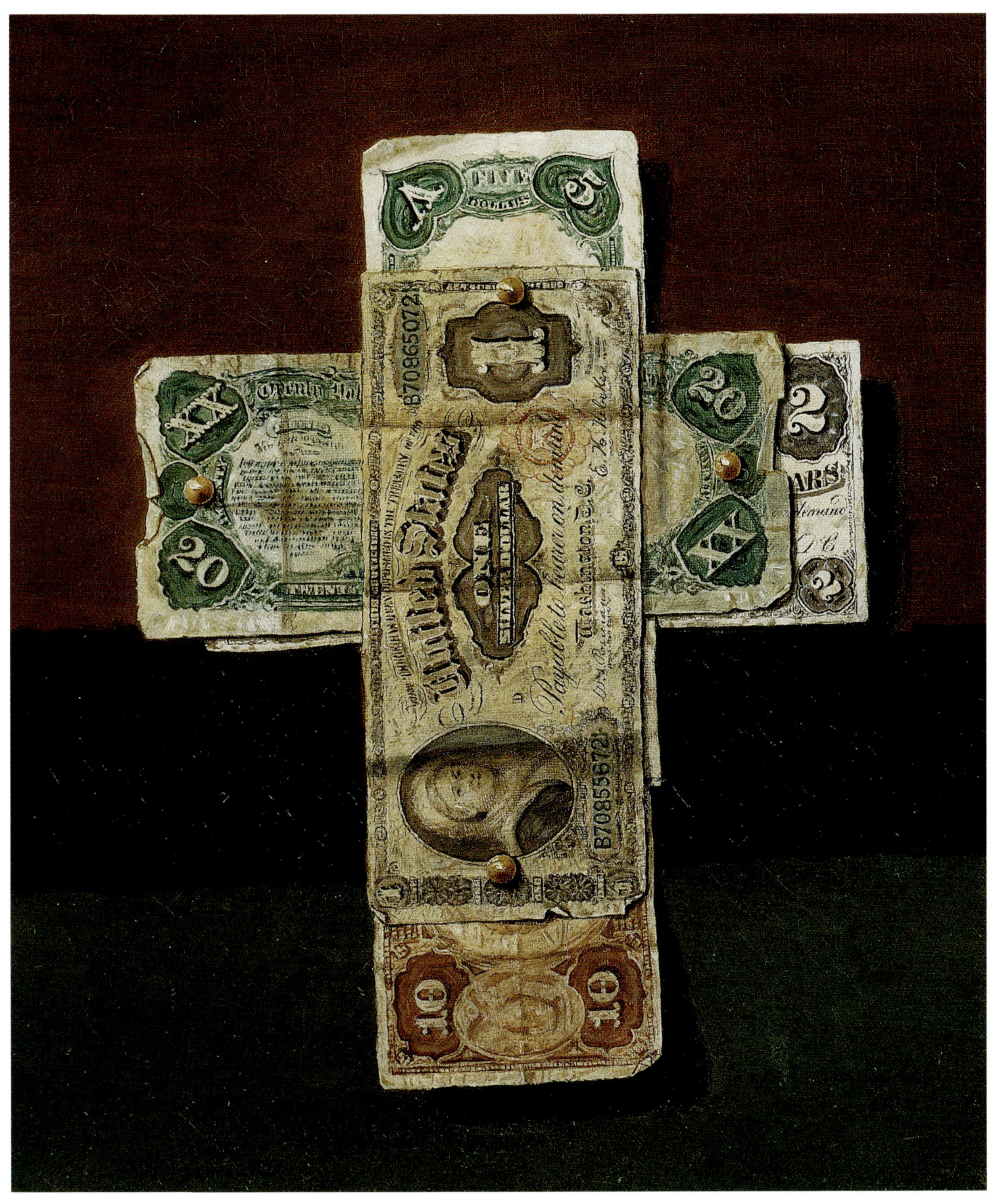

dard. In his speech, Bryan proclaimed: "Having behind us the commercial interests and the laboring interests and all the toiling masses, we shall answer their demands for a gold standard by saying to them, you shall not press down upon the brow of labor this crown of thorns. You shall not crucify mankind upon a cross of gold."[43]

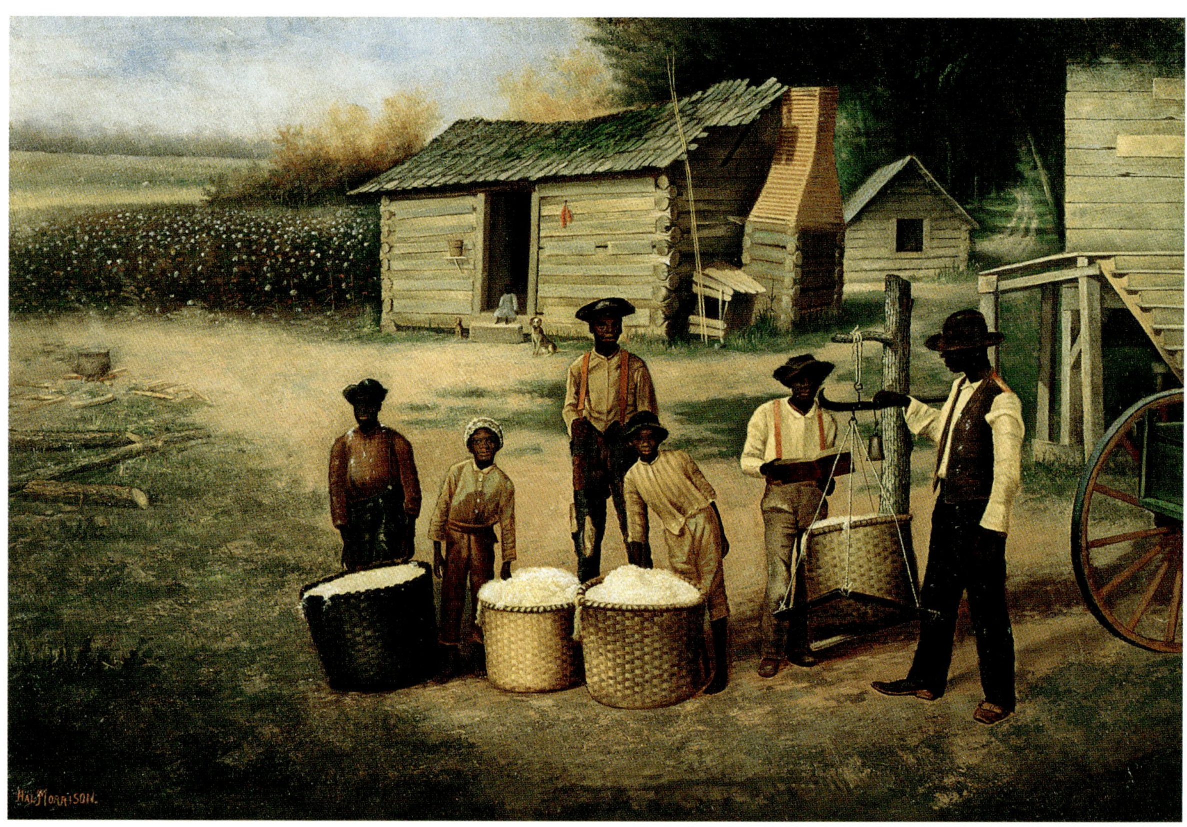

Figure 48
Hal Alexander Courtney Morrison, *Weighing the Cotton*, 1885–90, oil on canvas, 31½ x 45½ inches. Morris Museum of Art, Augusta, Georgia, 1989.01.123.
IN EXHIBITION

Although trompe l'oeil paintings, such as *Cross of Gold*, often appear perfectly neutral due to their inert subject matter and verisimilitude, there are reasons to believe that Dubreuil was sympathetic to Bryan's cause. Although little is known about his life, Dubreuil was described by those who knew him as poor.[44] As an impecunious, independent producer of goods he may have felt that his interests were aligned with those of farmers and artisans, who believed that enlarging the money supply would relieve their financial difficulties. Of the five bills in the painting, two are silver certificates and two are greenbacks, both types of currency that were favored by Populists and Democrats. The ten-dollar bill that describes the lower portion of the vertical bar of the cross is a National Bank Note. Neither greenback nor silver certificate, National Bank Notes were nonetheless an early attempt by the government to prevent money from concentrating in northeastern cities, particularly New York, by allowing local banks throughout the country to issue currency that was backed by specie in the United States Treasury. The circulation of multiple currencies was burdensome for artists, who had to judge the worth of their work in terms of values of money and commodities that shifted constantly. Thomas Waterman Wood's extensive account books show, for example, payment for his paintings in goods and services, in various banknotes backed by specie, in greenbacks, and even in gold.[45] Unfortunately for those desiring more comprehensive monetary reform through bimetallism, Bryan lost the presidency to McKinley.

Victor Dubreuil explored the complicated issue of national political economy in *Barrels of Money* and *Cross of Gold* at a time when American artists were developing entrepreneurial strategies to expand their market beyond their studios and traditional forms of patronage. In striving for financial autonomy, artists sought to prevent dealers and speculators from dictating the conditions under which art was bought and sold. Many of the tactics artists used to increase and control the market for American paintings can be correlated with the competitive behavior of men who were in the professions or were owners or managers of large, technologically dependent corporations—precisely the business elites who collected art.

The artists dispossessed of their studios in James Beard's and David Gilmour Blythe's paintings were evicted—as noted above—from the sites where they both produced and sold art (see figs. 32, 33). Throughout the 1860s, artists living in New York's Tenth Street Studio Building held well-attended receptions where the public thronged artists' work spaces and could mingle with, and buy from, the artist-residents.[46] As early as 1869, however, attendance at the receptions declined, and by 1878 Jervis McEntee could write in his diary about a conversation he had with a non-artist friend about the lack of visitors to his Tenth Street studio: "people had the greatest hesitancy about coming to artists' studios for fear of interrupting them. He seemed to think it quite surprising that I depend on selling my pictures to people who come to my room. The more I think of it the more I am convinced of the necessity of some business management for the sale of our pictures. The whole thing is changing. No one comes to the studios now."[47] Patrons ceased buying directly from artists' studios for several reasons. A critic in *The Galaxy* magazine believed that the novelty of the receptions had worn off and that elite New Yorkers were seeking new forms of entertainment. McEntee's view, that people did not want to interrupt artists in their studios, speaks to a growing emphasis on privacy in American culture; but it also suggests that art and artist alike were increasingly seen as occupying a realm set apart from the concerns of the workaday world. The comments of McEntee and the *Galaxy* critic also remind us that the venues for selling art were indeed in flux. The rise of department stores completed the shift, encouraging consumers to purchase goods in specialized retail environments such as commercial galleries and auction sales.[48]

As part of a "business management" strategy for the sale of their pictures, artists, in common with producers of agricultural and manufactured goods, took advantage of improvements in transportation to send their work to market at exhibitions and commercial galleries from New York to

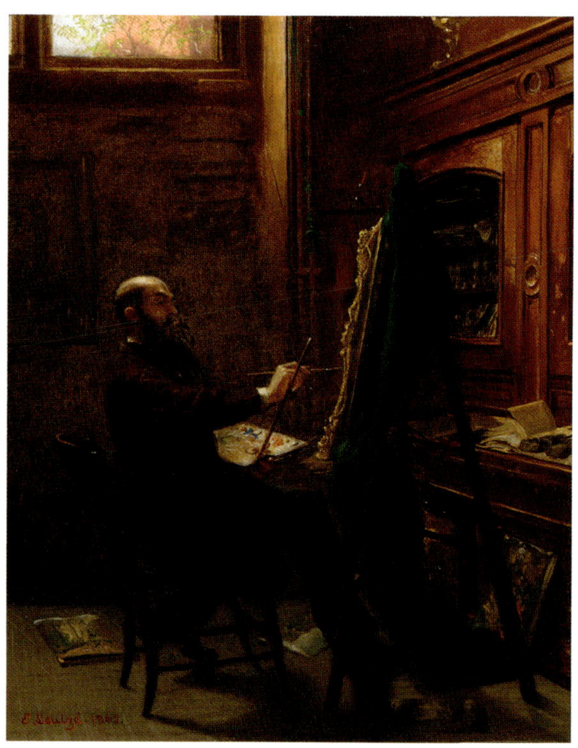

Figure 49
Emanuel Leutze, *Worthington Whittredge in His Tenth Street Studio*, 1865, oil on canvas, 15 x 12 inches. Reynolda House Museum of American Art, Winston-Salem, North Carolina. Gift of Barbara B. Millhouse, 1984.2.12.

San Francisco and in numerous smaller towns and cities in between, including Springfield, Massachusetts, Minneapolis, and Portland, Oregon. American artists also exhibited in large world's fairs and expositions held in both the United States and Europe, such as the Centennial Exhibition in Philadelphia in 1876; Universal Expositions in Paris in 1867, 1889, and 1900; and the World's Columbian Exposition in Chicago in 1893.[49]

The newly national scope of the market for American art presented economic challenges that artists responded to by forming corporations and consolidating power through mergers of their professional organizations. John Harrison Mills became involved in the New-York Art Union, an artist-run insurance corporation "formed to protect local artists when lending works for exhibition in other cities, not only from dishonest agents, but from losses on frames and canvasses while in transit . . . It also sees that artists are not defrauded of the sums paid for works sold in other cities" (see figs. 23, 34).[50] Through the Guild, Mills "developed and conducted a system of circuit exhibitions," indicating that the company began to integrate its insurance function with the creation of markets for its members' products, just as contemporary large corporations were also vertically integrating the production, distribution, and marketing of goods.[51]

In 1889, the New-York Art Guild, along with the Society of American Artists, Art Students' League, Architectural League, and Society of Painters in Pastel, incorporated as the American Fine Arts Society, erecting a building in New York where members of each of the founding organizations could exhibit their work. Board members, including Mills and J. Carroll Beckwith, noted that there were too few venues in the city for the display and sale of work by American artists. The society raised funds by selling $50,000 worth of stock to artists and $100 memberships to interested citizens, which would give them free admission for life to exhibitions and events in the building. Prominent members of the business community, including John D. Rockefeller, John Jacob Astor, Cornelius Vanderbilt II, George Vanderbilt, D. O. Mills, Levi P. Morton, and George Jay Gould, purchased memberships in the society. The merging of the five professional organizations with the stated aim of improving the market for American art came during a decade in which large corporations—including those run by American Fine Arts Society subscribers such as Rockefeller and the Vanderbilts—began to inte-

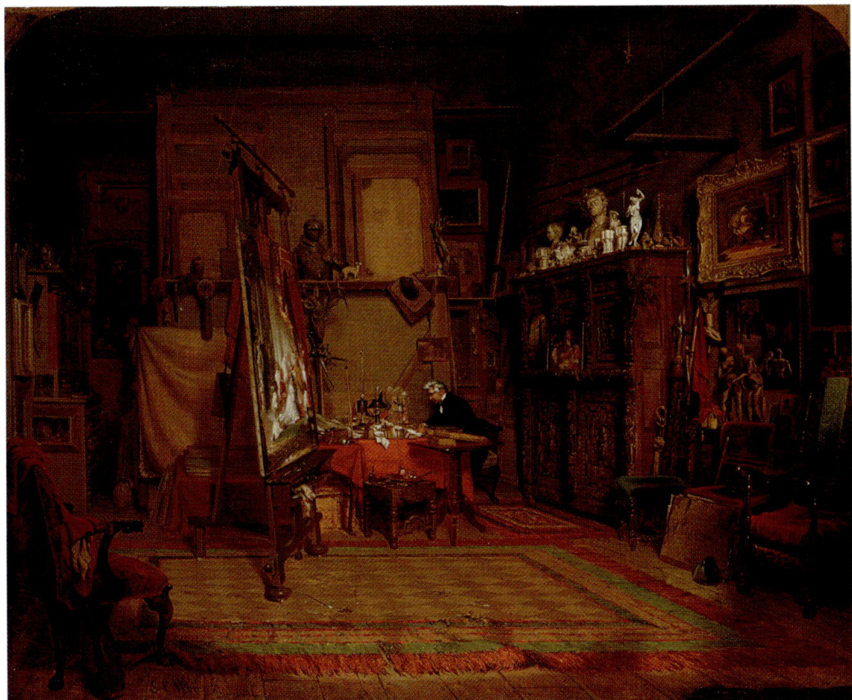

Figure 50
John Ferguson Weir, *An Artist's Studio*, 1864, oil on canvas, 25 1/2 x 30 1/2 inches. Los Angeles County Museum of Art. Gift of Jo Ann and Julian Ganz, Jr. (M.86.307). Digital Image © 2009 Museum Associates/LACMA/Art Resource, NY

grate horizontally through mergers to control the market for their products, often to the point of gaining monopoly power.[52] Artists believed that joining forces would benefit them as it did producers of oil or providers of transportation. To meet operating costs, the society would rent out its building at 215 West 57th Street for musical performances and exhibitions of art by nonmembers, but stipulated that no auctions were to be held there, a policy designed to prevent the kind of speculation by "collectors" such as Thomas B. Clarke and George Seney. For all of their efforts, however, the *New York Times* reported that the society did have to struggle to sell all of its stock "to hard-working artists . . . who have little pelf to spare."[53]

The American Fine Arts Society was one of a series of attempts by artists to create better economic conditions through cooperative action in professional organizations. In 1867, for example, members of the National Academy of Design lobbied Congress to raise the tariff on imported works of art from 10 percent to a flat $100, plus an additional 10 percent of each $1,000 in value. The Academy believed that this measure would stem what Jervis McEntee termed the "perfect deluge" of foreign paintings that American artists felt hurt their market. However, Congress failed to act on the academy's request.[54] In their support of a higher tariff, artists aligned their interests with those of American manufacturers who in the late nineteenth century supported the government's implementation of tariff rates between 40 and 50 percent of the dutiable value of many goods.[55]

Figure 51
William Merritt Chase, *The Inner Studio, Tenth Street*, 1882, oil on canvas, 32 3/8 x 44 1/4 inches. Huntington Library, Art Collections, and Botanical Gardens. Gift of the Virginia Steele Scott Foundation, 83.8.7.

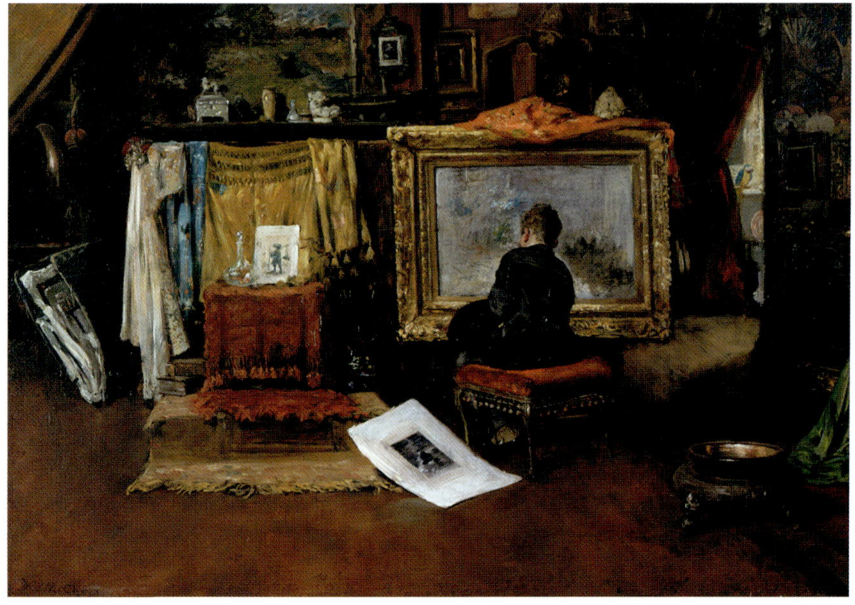

Artists involved in the incorporation of their industry portrayed themselves as sober professionals, surrounded by the tools of their trade. Emmanuel Leutze painted Worthington Whittredge, who would become President of the National Academy, in his studio at Tenth Street (1865; fig. 49). The neatly dressed and groomed artist is hard at work, and to his left is a cabinet filled with books and sketches from which he may draw inspiration. Similarly, Robert Walter Weir, father of J. Alden Weir (see fig. 37), is barely visible at a table in the back of his cavernous studio, surrounded by the materials from which he created precisely detailed history paintings such as *The Embarkation of the Pilgrims* for the United States Capitol (fig. 50).[56] William Merritt Chase depicted a male figure, whose identity remains ambiguous, before a painting in Chase's famous studio in the Tenth Street Building (fig. 51). In Chase's case, the bric-a-brac that filled his large studio served less as inspiration than as expression of his exquisite and cosmopolitan taste, the fine aesthetic sensibility that made him a great artist.[57] Chase was a founding member of the Society of American Artists, a competitor to the National Academy and one of four organizations that combined to form the American Fine Arts Society. Chase also helped incorporate the New-York Art Guild.[58] These three images of artists' working environments more closely resemble portraits of lawyers, doctors, or scientists, such as Thomas Eakins's painting of physicist Henry Rowland (1897; fig. 52), than the self-portraits by Blythe, Beard, or Ryder.

Although American artists embraced entrepreneurial strategies modeled after big business, many continued to celebrate artisans and pre-corporate

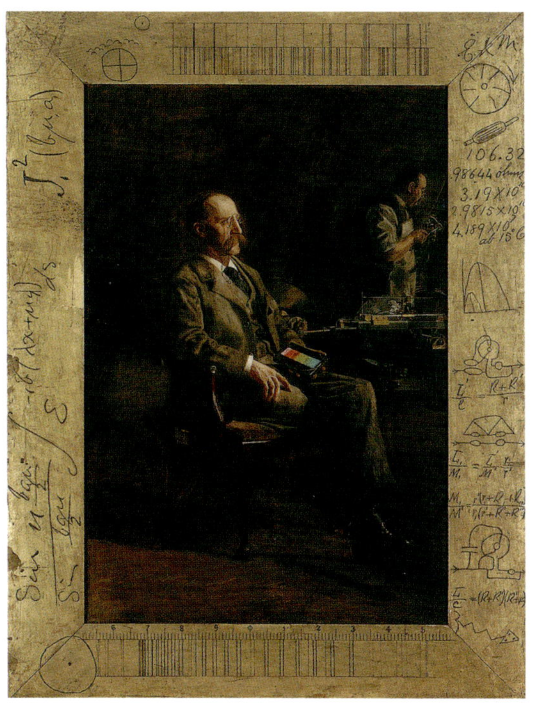

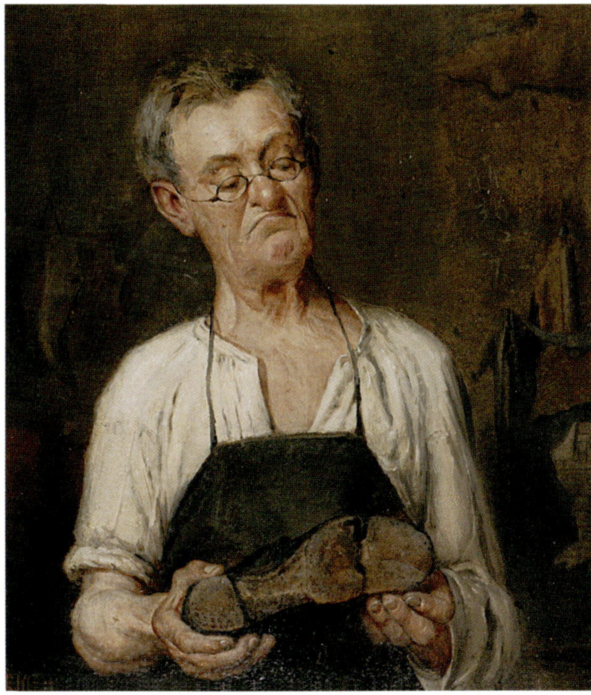

methods of exchange. The Washington, D.C.–based Frank Moss, who studied in Paris under Léon Bonnat, created in *A Difficult Job* (n.d.) a humorous but poignant image of a cobbler who gazes quizzically from the canvas toward the viewer while presenting the sole of a shoe that has seen better days (fig. 53). Perhaps tellingly, his frown repeats the arc of the shoe, as if the former is the result of his unrelenting labor on the latter. The painting arouses sympathy for the difficult task awaiting the artisan, but also for the owner of the shoe, whose financial circumstances forced him to repair the completely worn-out footwear rather than replace it. Thomas Waterman Wood, who as president of the National Academy from 1891 to 1899 directed the largest corporate body of American artists, painted a scene of barter in *The Yankee Pedlar* (1872; fig. 54). The merchant displays his pushcart of fabrics, housewares, and tools to a rural family who has brought goods from the farm, including eggs, to trade for produce. Early in his career, Wood bartered paintings for a brocade dress for his own wife and for the services of a cobbler like the one Moss portrayed in *A Difficult Job*—he traded two portraits in return for new boots and the repair of old ones.[59] By the last third of the nineteenth century, however, New York City had outlawed the kind of pushcarts Wood depicted, causing acrimony between city government and the laboring classes, who both operated and patronized the carts.[60]

Three trompe l'oeil paintings created in Philadelphia—William Harnett's *Job Lot Cheap* (1878), John Frederick Peto's *Job Lot Cheap* (1892), and Peto's

Figure 52
Thomas Eakins, *Professor Henry A. Rowland*, 1897, oil on canvas, 80¼ x 54 inches. Addison Gallery of American Art, Phillips Academy, Andover, Massachusetts. Gift of Stephen C. Clarke, Esq., 1931.5. Photo: Greg Heins.

Figure 53
Frank Moss, *A Difficult Job*, n.d., oil on walnut panel, 8⅝ x 7⅛ inches. State Museum of Pennsylvania, Pennsylvania Historical and Museum Commission, Transfer from Hope Lodge, 75.1.
IN EXHIBITION

Figure 54
Thomas Waterman Wood, *The Yankee Pedlar*, 1872, oil on canvas, 28 x 40 inches. Terra Foundation for American Art, Chicago, Daniel J. Terra Art Acquisition Endowment Fund, 1998.3. Photo: Terra Foundation for American Art, Chicago/Art Resource, NY.
IN EXHIBITION

Figure 55 (opposite)
William M. Harnett, *Job Lot Cheap*, 1878, oil on canvas, 18 x 36 inches. Reynolda House Museum of American Art, Winston-Salem, North Carolina. Original purchase fund from the Mary Reynolds Babcock Foundation, Z. Smith Reynolds Foundation, ARCA Foundation, and Anne Cannon Forsyth, 1966.2.10.
IN EXHIBITION

Figure 56 (opposite)
Rose Hartwell, *A Corner Window in a Pawn Shop*, 1893, oil on canvas, 34 1/8 x 28 3/16 inches.
Brigham Young University Museum of Art, Inv. No. 820046706.
Photo: Courtesy of Brigham Young University Museum of Art.
IN EXHIBITION

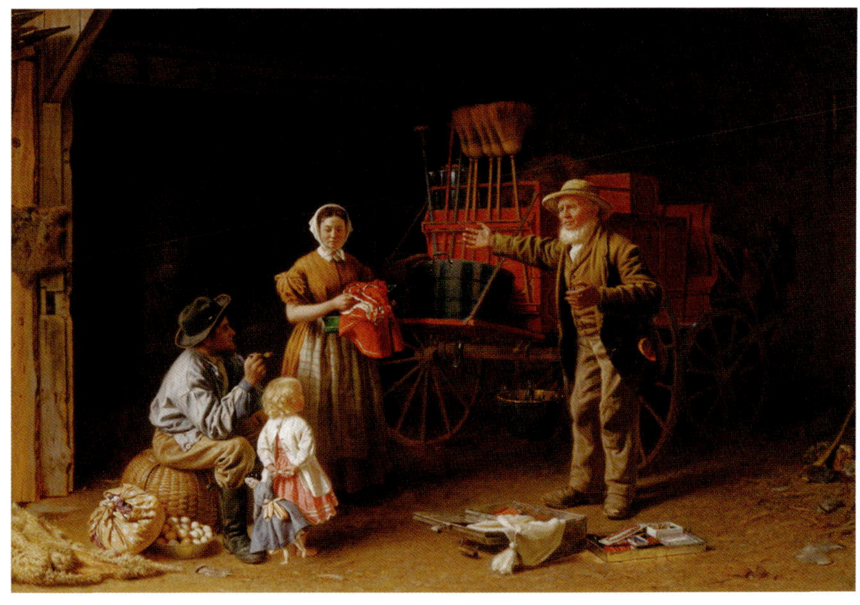

Poor Man's Store (1885)—also look back to outmoded forms of commerce (figs. 55, 57, and 58). As art historian Andrew Walker has observed, discriminating nineteenth-century customers, increasingly accustomed to uniformly bound books offered at standard prices, would have disdained the motley assortment of books Harnett shows, a job lot in various states of disrepair awaiting purchase by some enterprising merchant.[61] In Peto's rendering, the same subject is even more abject, due to its notice of rooms for rent and its date of 1892, fourteen years after Harnett's painting, which suggests that for many, economic conditions did not improve as the nineteenth century waned. The remnants of a red cardstock sign tacked to the upper left corner of the open shutter perhaps indicated the name and occupation of a former tenant off to seek his or her fortune elsewhere, whether willingly or not, as in the case of Blythe's and Beard's artists. The enterprising proprietor of the *Poor Man's Store* offers room and board in addition to homemade sweets, fruit, and peanuts. It is tempting to link the artist's experiences trying to earn a livelihood with the subject of his painting: Peto had trouble selling his work in Philadelphia and was constantly moving the location of his studio. Shortly after painting the *Poor Man's Store* he vacated Philadelphia for good, settling in New Jersey. There, he tried to sell his paintings at the local drugstore and supplemented the meager proceeds by playing the coronet at Christian revival meetings.[62] All three paintings reveal that the struggle to make ends meet—to sell anything—led small-scale merchants to deal in tattered goods that could scarcely be considered commodities.

Although far removed from Harnett's and Peto's verisimilitude, Rose Hartwell's *A Corner Window in a Pawn Shop* (1893) similarly depicts goods

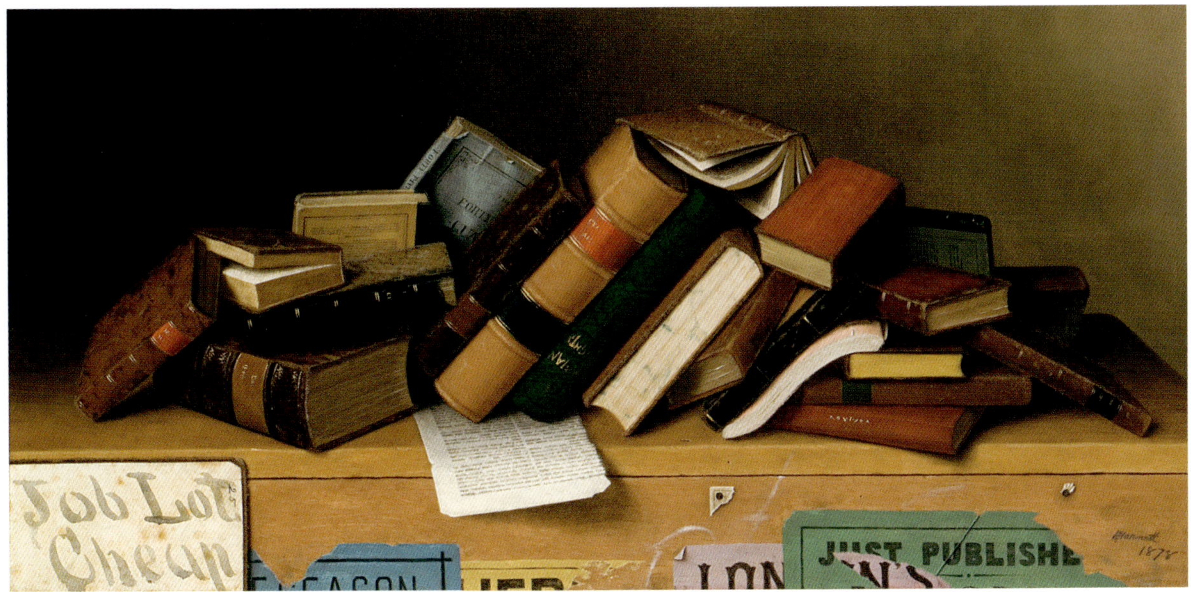

at the bottom of the commercial food chain (fig. 56). The painting, with its artful composition of jewelry, watches, and objets d'art unified through a harmonious color palette, initially appears to be an exercise in aesthetics influenced by the work of artists such as Whistler and Chase. However, its subject and the date of the work, 1893—the beginning of the most severe depression in the nineteenth century—point to financial trauma. The work's emphasis on the decorative aspects of painting distances the viewer from the personal fiscal tragedies that brought the sundry objects to the pawnshop.

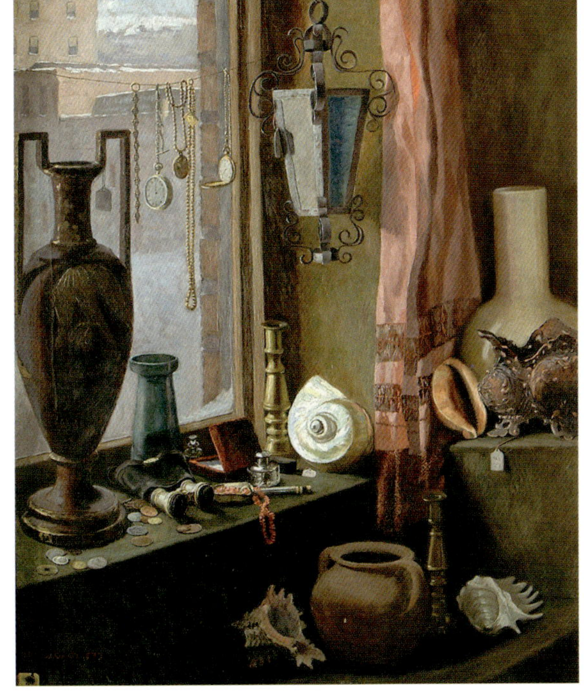

Evidence suggests that the entrepreneurial strategies of artists did benefit the market for their work. The average real price for paintings by American artists rose during the late nineteenth century, even though the economy as a whole saw deflation. A survey of over 1,500 genre paintings, including examples by Thomas Waterman Wood, James Beard, Charles Blauvelt, John George Brown, E. L. Henry, and Eastman Johnson, shows that the average price per painting increased from $105 in the 1850s to $555 in the 1890s. Even a work dealing with monetary uncertainty, such as Wood's *A Doubtful Coin* (1881; private collection), a work very similar to Charles Blauvelt's painting of the same subject (fig. 59), sold for a respectable $608. The average price of a painting

Figure 57
John Frederick Peto, *Job Lot Cheap*, 1892, oil on canvas, 29 5/8 x 39 3/4 inches. Fine Arts Museums of San Francisco. Gift of Mr. and Mrs. John D. Rockefeller 3rd, 1979.7.81.

Figure 58 (opposite)
John Frederick Peto, *The Poor Man's Store*, 1885, oil on canvas and panel, 35 1/2 x 25 5/8 inches. Museum of Fine Arts, Boston. Gift of Maxim Karolik for the M. and M. Karolik Collection of American Paintings, 1815–1865, 62.278.

Figure 59 (opposite)
Charles F. Blauvelt, *At the Grocer's*, also called *The Doubtful Bill*, 1889, oil on canvas, 24 x 20 inches. Collection of Mr. and Mrs. Thomas Davies.
IN EXHIBITION

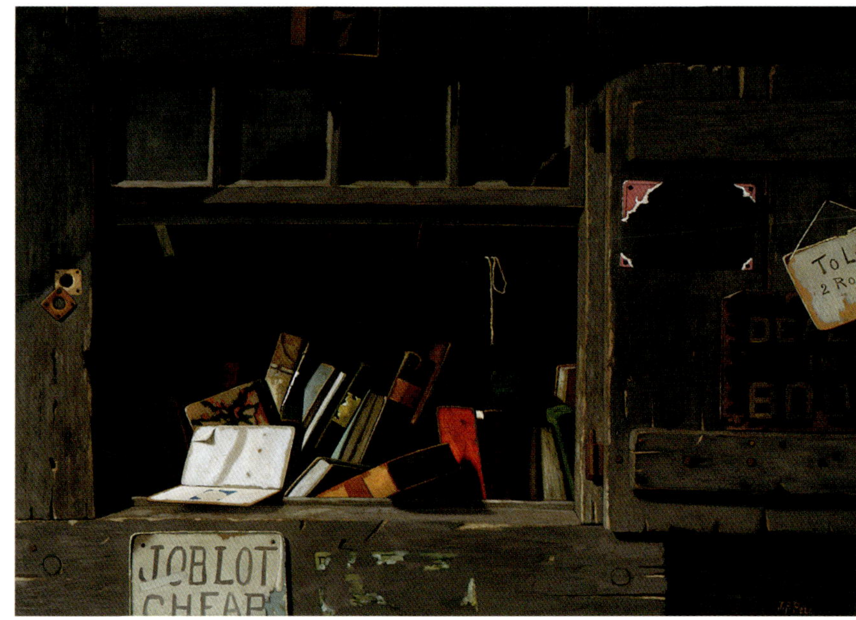

by artists working in Tonalist and Impressionist styles, including Albert Ryder, James Whistler, and George Inness, rose from $210 in the 1870s to $830 in the 1890s.[63]

Although James Inglis quoted Ryder as saying "sometimes poverty is a blessing," he sold paintings for prices in the thousands of dollars, such as the $3,500 Charles Wood paid for Ryder's *Jonah* (ca. 1885–95; Smithsonian American Art Museum). After the Thomas B. Clarke sale, where Ryder's paintings commanded some of the top prices, the artist had "clients visiting him daily and offering commissions and even money." One such new client was Dr. Albert T. Sanden, original owner of *The Poor Artist*, described by Ryder as "a very nice and just man. He comes to my studio . . . and is trying to coax me to make $20,000 in work this year."[64] As noted above, Ryder hatched a scheme to turn his profits from painting into stock so that he could live on the dividends. Other artists, including J. Carroll Beckwith, Albert Bierstadt, and Winslow Homer, did invest in property and securities. Even Jervis McEntee and Worthington Whittredge, who were clearly pessimistic about the economic prospects for American art, kept studios at the Tenth Street Studio Building and homes in the country where they supported extended families. John George Brown confided to McEntee that he sold $3,000 worth of paintings in the winter of 1876–77, a period when the average annual income was approximately $400.[65] As we have seen, J. Carroll Beckwith expressed his guilt at spending $18 on a dinner with friends at a time when the average farmhand made just $13.93 per month, including board.[66]

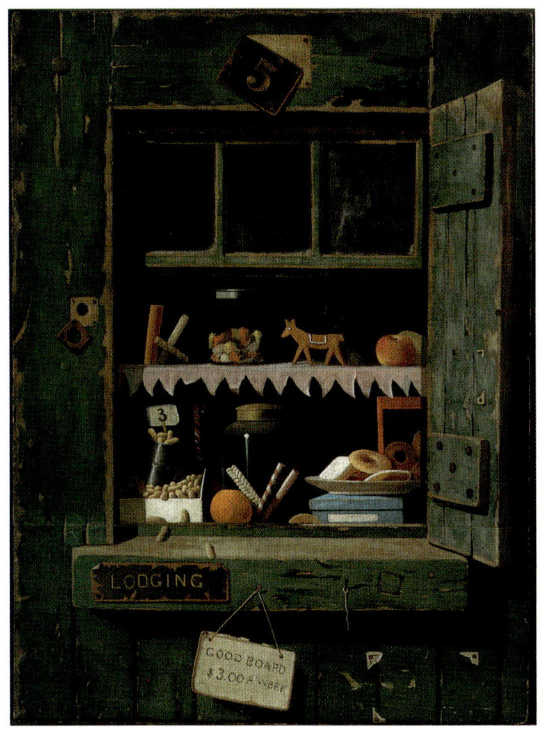

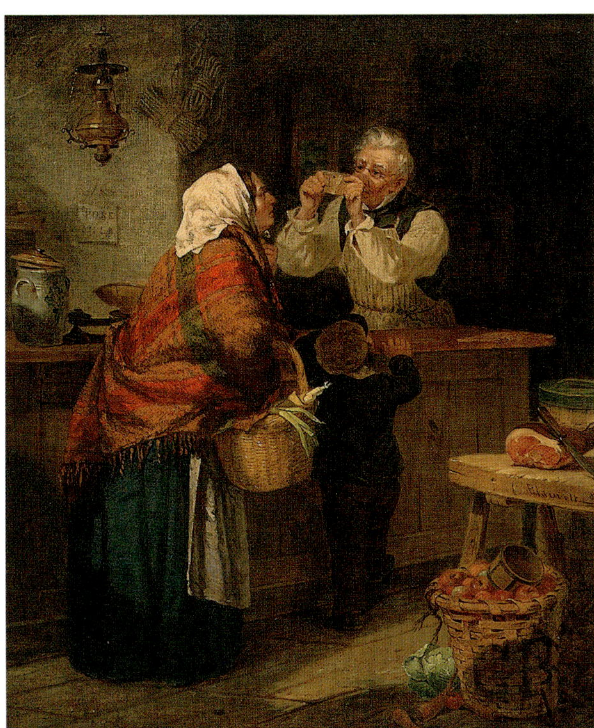

There seems then to be a contradiction—real and imagined—between the income of Albert Pinkham Ryder and his representation in *The Poor Artist* (see fig. 35). This contradiction is also manifest in comparing the down-and-out artists in David Gilmour Blythe's *Art Versus Law* and James Beard's *Studio to Let* with the dapper, bourgeois practitioners in Leutze's *Worthington Whittredge in His Tenth Street Studio* and John Ferguson Weir's depiction of his father Robert Weir's studio (figs. 32, 33, 49, 50). All four paintings date from the early 1860s, heightening the apparent discrepancy. Regional factors explain some of the difference, as money tended to collect in the large cities of the northeast, particularly New York. Blythe and Beard worked in Pittsburgh and Cincinnati respectively, whereas Whittredge and Ryder, in New York, had better access to venues for the sale of their work, including the National Academy, gentlemen's clubs, and the nascent system of commercial galleries. However, as I have emphasized throughout this essay, artists in New York also complained—sometimes bitterly—of financial problems and strategized ways to improve the market for their work.

Artists' rhetoric of poverty, even while some made a decent income, and the disparate economic circumstances of Beard, Blythe, Ryder, Whittredge, and Weir all speak to turmoil in the American economy. Paintings in this exhibition, including Charles Blauvelt's *At the Grocer's* (also called *The Doubtful Bill*; see fig. 59), demonstrate socioeconomic realities that artists and their contemporaries experienced daily, if not always firsthand, in city streets, the popular press, and novels such as William Dean Howell's *A Hazard of New Fortunes* (1890) or Stephen Crane's *Maggie, a Girl of the Streets* (1896). The artists in this exhibition explored the vagaries of an economy plagued by poverty and inequality, made even worse by the panics of the late nineteenth century. Their works show how tenuous financial security was for nearly everyone in late nineteenth-century America, whether artist, farmer, or even Wall Street speculator. In 1865, William Sidney Mount, speaking about the anxieties of his profession, could proclaim but one constant form of wealth: "The painter with but a little money has one consolation, he owns all his eyes take in—the riches of sight."[67]

1. See Sarah Burns, *Painting the Dark Side: Art and the Gothic Imagination in Nineteenth-Century America* (Berkeley: University of California Press, 2004), 44–45; and Bruce Chambers, *The World of David Gilmour Blythe* (Washington, D.C.: National Collection of Fine Arts and Smithsonian Institution Press, 1980), 75.

2. On links between this painting and critiques of the income tax by Mills's colleague Mark Twain, see Joyce Henri Robertson et al., *An Endless Panorama of Beauty: Selections from the Jean and Alvin Snowiss Collection of American Art* (University Park, Pa.: Palmer Museum of Art in association with the Pennsylvania State University Press, 2003), 79.

3. At the National Academy, the leading artists' professional organization in the United States in the nineteenth century, paintings marked with a "2" were those favored by most—but not all—members of the committee charged with selecting works for the group's important annual exhibitions. See Bennard Perlman, *Painters of the Ashcan School: The Immortal Eight* (New York: Dover, 1979), 127.

4. Elizabeth Broun, *Albert Pinkham Ryder* (Washington, D.C.: Smithsonian Institution Press, 1989), 135–39.

5. William I. Homer, "A Group of Paintings and Drawings by Ryder," *Record of the Art Museum, Princeton University* 18, no. 1 (1959): 25.

6. Henry Eckford [pseudo. Charles de Kay], "A Modern Colorist," *Century Magazine* 40 (June 1890): 252–53. See also William Innes Homer and Lloyd Goodrich, *Albert Pinkham Ryder, Painter of Dreams* (New York: Abrams, 1989), 90–94; and Homer, "A Group of Paintings and Drawings by Ryder," 25.

7. Jervis McEntee to James Pinchot, June 25, 1876; Gifford Pinchot Papers, Library of Congress, Washington, D.C. (hereafter Pinchot Papers).

8. On changes to the structure of the American art market, see Linda Henefield Skalet, "The Market for American Painting in New York: 1870–1915" (PhD diss., Johns Hopkins University, 1980); Madeline Fidell Beaufort and Jeanne K. Welcher, "Some Views of Art Buying in New York in the 1870s and 1880s," *Oxford Art Journal* 5, no. 1 (1982): 48–49; Lois Marie Fink, "French Art in the United States, 1850–1870: Three Dealers and Collectors," *Gazette des Beaux Arts* 92, ser. 6 (September 1978): 87–100; Annette Blaugrund, *The Tenth Street Studio Building: Artist-Entrepreneurs from the Hudson River to the American Impressionists* (Seattle: University of Washington Press, 1997); Kevin M. Murphy, "Economics of Style: The Business Practices of American Artists and the Structure of the Market 1850–1910" (PhD diss., University of California, Santa Barbara, 2005); and John Ott, "How New York Stole the Luxury Art Market: Blockbuster Auctions and Bourgeois Identity in Gilded Age America," *Winterthur Portfolio* 42 (Summer/Autumn 2008): 133–58.

9. Worthington Whittredge to James Pinchot, February 15, 1874; Pinchot Papers.

10. J. Carroll Beckwith, diary entry June 7, 1895; J. Carroll Beckwith Papers, Archives of American Art, Smithsonian Institution, Washington, D.C., reel 800 (hereafter Beckwith Papers).

11. J. Carroll Beckwith, diary entry June 3, 1895; Beckwith Papers.

12. Chales W. Calomiris and Larry Schweikart, "The Panic of 1857: Origins, Transmission, and Containment," *Journal of Economic History* 51, no. 4 (December 1991): 807–34; and Robert Sobel, *Panic on Wall Street: A History of America's Financial Disasters* (Washington, D.C.: Beard Books, 1999), 104.

13. Grace Mayer, "A Painting of the 'Revulsion' of 1857," *Bulletin of the Museum of the City of New York* 3 (May 1940): 71.

14. See Alan Trachtenberg, *The Incorporation of America: Culture and Society in the Gilded Age* (New York: Hill and Wang, 1982), 70–100.

15. *Fifteenth Annual Report of the New York Association for Improving the Conditions of the Poor*, 1858, p. 19; quoted in Samuel Rezeneck, *Business Depressions and Financial Panics: Essays in American Business and Economic History* (New York: Greenwood Publishing Corporation, 1968), 22. Vanderbilt's membership is recorded in the *Thirty-Sixth Annual Report of the New York Association for Improving the Conditions of the Poor*, 1879, pp. 43 and 95. http://books.google.com.

16. Sven Beckert, *The Monied Metropolis: New York City and the Consolidation of the American Bourgeoisie*, 1850–1896 (New York: Cambridge University Press, 1993), 217.

17. Sobel, *Panic on Wall Street*, 137–53.

18. Henry Adams, "The New York Gold Conspiracy," in Adams, *Historical Essays* (New York: Scribner's, 1891), 318.

19. David Stewart Hull, *James Henry Cafferty*, N.A. (New York: New-York Historical Society, 1986), 33.

20. Beckwith, Properties January 1, 1896; Beckwith Papers.

21. "Albert Bierstadt's Schedules," *New York Times*, February 14, 1895, p. 4.

22. James Inglis to C.E.S. Wood, November 15, 1895; Wood Papers.

23. Winslow Homer to J. Eastman Chase, March 5, 1882; J. Eastman Chase Papers, Archives of American Art, Smithsonian Institution, Washington, D.C., reel 996, frames 217–18. For Homer's engagement in the marketing of his work, see Kevin M. Murphy, "Painting for Money: Winslow Homer as Entrepreneur," *Winterthur Portfolio* 37 (Summer/Autumn 2002): 147–60.

24. Winslow Homer to M. Knoedler and Co., September 24, 1903; Winslow Homer Letters, in Winslow Homer Papers, Archives of American Art, Smithsonian Institution, Washington, D.C., reel NY59-5 (hereafter Homer Papers), frame 395.

25. James Inglis to C. E. S. Wood, June 15, 1897; Charles Erskine Scott Wood Papers, The Huntington Library, Art Collections, and Botanical Gardens (hereafter Wood Papers).

26. Clarence Cook, "The Cry from the Studios," *The Galaxy*, February 15, 1867, p. 435.

27. Homer to Knoedler, January 28, 1901; Homer Papers, frames 422–24.

28. For a positive view of Clarke's activities in promoting American art, see H. Barbara Weinberg, "Thomas B. Clarke, Foremost Patron of American Art from 1872 to 1899," *American Art Journal* 8 (May 1976): 52–83.

29. Inglis to C. E. S. Wood, February 25, 1899; Wood Papers. Although Clarke did some good for American art, he did speculate in paintings. After the 1899 auction he amassed a collection of Colonial and Federal portraits that he put on the block in 1913.

30. Weinberg, "Thomas B. Clarke," 77–78.

31. Montague Marks, "My Note Book," *Art Amateur* 30 (March 1894): 98. In this case Clarke's judgment did not pay off. He paid $850 for the Johnson in 1891 but it fetched only $800 in 1899; Weinberg, "Thomas B. Clarke," 78.

32. Trachtenberg, *Incorporation of America*, 99.

33. Inglis to C. E. S. Wood, November 15, 1895; Wood Papers.

34. Albert Pinkham Ryder to William Macbeth; Macbeth Gallery Papers, Archives of American Art, Smithsonian Institution, Washington, D.C., reel 2629, frame 603. Ryder was upset that Macbeth wanted to clean one of his paintings, which Ryder believed would damage it.

35. C. E. S. Wood to J. Alden Weir, July 7, 1899; Wood Papers.

36. In addition to his essay here, see also Leo Mazow, "George Inness, Henry George, the Single Tax, and the Future Poet," *American Art* 18 (Spring 2004): 60–77.

37. Edward J. Nygren, "The Almighty Dollar: Money as a Theme in American Painting," *Winterthur Portfolio* 23 (Summer/Autumn 1988): 129–50; and Bruce Chambers, *Old Money: Trompe L'Oeil Images of Currency* (New York: Berry-Hill Galleries, 1988).

38. Chambers, *Old Money*, 76. See also Nygren, "Almighty Dollar," 143. On the monopolistic strategies of big business, see Alfred D. Chandler's *The Visible Hand: The Managerial Revolution in American Business* (Cambridge, Mass.: Belknap Press of Harvard University Press, 1977).

39. Alfred Frankenstein, *After the Hunt*, rev. ed. (Berkeley: University of California Press, 1963), 151. See also Nygren, "Almighty Dollar," 135; and Chambers, *Old Money*, 22–23, 76.

40. Gretchen Ritter, *Goldbugs and Greenbacks: The Antimonopoly Tradition and the Politics of Finance in America 1865–1896* (New York: Cambridge University Press, 1997), 74–75.

41. For a concise summary of farmers' problems due to contraction of the money supply, see Lawrence Goodwyn, *Democratic Promise: The Populist Movement in America* (New York: Oxford University Press, 1976), 11–15, 26–31. A more nuanced view can be found in Ritter, *Goldbugs and Greenbacks*, 196–98.

42. This is an extreme simplification of a highly complex issue. While Ritter suggested in *Goldbugs and Greenbacks* (p. 154) that many who had supported the fiat legal tender of greenbacks became supporters of free silver, Lawrence Goodwyn, in *Democratic Promise*, delineated the opposition between "greenbackers" and "silverites" (pp. 426–36).

43. William Jennings Bryan, *The First Battle: A Story of the Campaign of 1896* (Chicago: W. B. Conkey, 1896), 206.

44. Chambers, *Old Money*, 67.

45. See, for example, account book entries for February 28, 1860; April 7, 1860; April 13, 1861; and May 24, 1862; Thomas Waterman Wood Papers, Archives of American Art, Smithsonian Institution, Washington, D.C. (hereafter T. W. Wood Papers), reel 2809.

46. On the receptions, see Blaugrund, *Tenth Street Studio*.

47. James McEntee diary, February 13, 1878; Jervis McEntee Papers, Archives of American Art, Smithsonian Institution, Washington, D.C. (hereafter McEntee Papers), reel D180, frame 190.

48. "The Studio Receptions," *The Galaxy* 7 (February 1869): 301; John Kasson, *Rudeness and Civility: Manners in Nineteenth-Century America* (New York: Hill and Wang, 1990), 170–71; Lawrence Levine, *Highbrow Lowbrow: The Emergence of Cultural Hierarchy in America* (Cambridge, Mass.: Harvard University Press, 1986), 146–68; and Trachtenberg, *Incorporation of America*, 130–34.

49. On American art at the numerous world's fairs, see Carol Troyen, "Innocents Abroad: American Painters at the 1867 Exposition Universelle, Paris," *American Art Journal* 16 (Autumn 1984): 2–29; Kimberly Orcutt, "'Revising History': Creating a Canon of American Art at the Centennial Exhibition" (PhD diss., City University of New York, 2005); Annette Blaugrund, et al., *Paris 1889: American Artists at the Universal Exposition* (Philadelphia: Pennsylvania Academy of the Fine Arts, 1989); Carolyn Kinder Carr, *Revisiting the White City: American Art at the 1893 World's Fair* (Washington, D.C.: National Museum of

American Art and National Portrait Gallery, Smithsonian Institution, 1993); and Diane P. Fischer, ed., *Paris 1900: The "American School" at the Universal Exposition* (New Brunswick, N.J.: Montclair Art Museum, 1999).

50. "The Fine Arts Society," *New York Times*, January 4, 1890, p. 4. On the incorporation of the New-York Art Union, see "Art Notes," *The Critic* 15 (February 28, 1891): 160.

51. John Harrison Mills, autobiographical note, *Express* (Buffalo, N.Y.), November 5, 1916; quoted in Robert Taft, *Artists and Illustrators of the Old West, 1850–1900* (New York: Scribner's, 1953), 346. On vertical integration of manufacturers into marketing, see Chandler, *Visible Hand*, 302–12.

52. Chandler, *Visible Hand*, 320–31.

53. "The Fine Arts Society"; see also "A New Art Project," *New York Times*, October 4, 1889, p. 9; "Only a Little Delay, Officers of the American Fine Arts Society Deny a Rumor," *New York Times*, November 24, 1889, p. 11; and "A Proposed New Art Building," *The Critic* 11 (June 22, 1889): 311–12.

54. McEntee diary, November 11, 1872; McEntee Papers, frame 13. On tariff rates for imported art, see William J. Barber, "International Commerce in the Fine Arts and the American Political Economy," in Neil de Marchi and Crawfurd W. Goodwin, eds., *Economic Engagements with Art* (Durham, N.C.: Duke University Press, 1999), 209–34.

55. W. Elliot Brownlee, *Federal Taxation in America: A Short History*, 2nd ed. (Washington, D.C.: Woodrow Wilson Center Press; Cambridge: Cambridge University Press, 2004), 36–37.

56. Ilene Susan Fort and Michael Quick, *American Art: A Catalogue of the Los Angeles County Museum of Art* (Los Angeles: The Museum, 1991), 132–34.

57. On Chase's studio, see Blaugrund, *Tenth Street Studio Building*; and Sarah Burns, *Inventing the Modern Artist: Art and Culture in Gilded Age America* (New Haven: Yale University Press, 1996), 67–74.

58. "Art Notes," *The Critic* 15 (March 21, 1891): 160.

59. Account book entries, February 5 and September 1, 1853; T. W. Wood Papers.

60. David C. Hammack, *Power and Society: Greater New York at the Turn of the Century* (New York: Russell Sage Foundation, 1982), 137–38. See also Beckert, *The Monied Metropolis*, 316.

Exhibition Checklist

1. James Henry Beard (1811–1893)
   Studio to Let, 1864
   Oil on canvas
   16 5/8 × 13 3/4 inches
   Herbert F. Johnson Museum of Art, Cornell University
   Acquired through the Ernest I. White, Class of 1893, Endowment Fund

2. Charles F. Blauvelt (1824–1900)
   At the Grocer's, also called *The Doubtful Bill*, 1889
   Oil on canvas
   24 × 20 inches
   Collection of Mr. and Mrs. Thomas Davies

3. David Gilmour Blythe (1815–1865)
   Art versus Law, 1859–60
   Oil on canvas
   24 × 35 13/16 inches
   Brooklyn Museum
   Dick Ramsay Fund, 40.907

4. David Gilmour Blythe (1815–1865)
   A Match Seller, ca. 1859
   Oil on canvas
   27 × 22 inches
   North Carolina Museum of Art
   Purchased with funds from the State of North Carolina

5. John George Brown (1831–1913)
   Buy a Posy, 1886
   Oil on canvas
   23 1/8 × 15 1/8 inches
   North Carolina Museum of Art
   Given in memory of Mr. and Mrs. E. J. Ellisberg by their children

6. James Henry Cafferty (1819–1869)
   The Weary Newsboy, 1861
   Oil on canvas
   12 3/8 × 9 7/8 inches
   Palmer Museum of Art, The Pennsylvania State University
   Purchased with funds from the Terra Art Enrichment Fund, 2003.23

7. James Henry Cafferty (1819–1869)
   Charles G. Rosenberg (1818–1879)
   Wall Street, Half Past Two O'Clock, October 13, 1857, 1858
   Oil on canvas
   50 × 40 inches
   Museum of the City of New York
   Gift of the Honorable Irwin Untermeyer, 40.54

8. William de la Montagne Cary (1840–1922)
   Pike's Peak or Bust, early 1870s
   Oil on canvas
   21 × 36 inches
   Hood Museum of Art, Dartmouth College
   Purchased through the Guernsey Center Moore 1904 Memorial Fund

9. Cassius Marcellus Coolidge (1844–1934)
   Edwin Austin Abbey (1852–1911)
   "Hard Times": Mortgaging the Old Homestead, 1873
   Engraving
   Harper's Weekly Magazine 17 (June 21, 1873)
   The Pennsylvania State University Libraries (venue 1)
   The Huntington Library, Art Collections, and Botanical Gardens (venue 2)

10. Victor Dubreuil (active, 1886–ca. 1900)
The Cross of Gold, ca. 1896
Oil on canvas
14 × 12 inches
Private collection
Courtesy of Berry-Hill Galleries, New York

11. Stanley Fox (active late 1860s)
Evading the Excise Law—Laying in Rum for Sunday, 1868
Engraving
Harper's Weekly Magazine 11 (February 6, 1867)
The Pennsylvania State University Libraries (venue 1)
The Huntington Library, Art Collections, and Botanical Gardens (venue 2)

12. William M. Harnett (1848–1892)
Job Lot Cheap, 1878
Oil on canvas
18 × 36 inches
Reynolda House Museum of American Art, Winston-Salem, North Carolina
Original purchase fund from the Mary Reynolds Babcock Foundation, Z. Smith Reynolds Foundation, ARCA Foundation, and Anne Cannon Forsyth, 1966.2.10

13. Rose Hartwell (1861–1917)
A Corner Window in a Pawn Shop, 1893
Oil on canvas
34 1/8 × 28 3/16 inches
Brigham Young University Museum of Art, Provo, Utah

14. Edward Lamson Henry (1841–1919)
Capital and Labor, 1881
Oil on canvas
12 1/2 × 15 3/8 inches
New-York Historical Society
Gift of George A. Zabriskie, 1940.5

15. Henry Hutt (1875–1950)
My Dear Kate, You Have No Idea How Hard Put to It I Am to Make Ends Meet. I Am So Poor It Is a Scandal, 1899
Gouache on illustration board
25 13/16 x 19 7/8 inches
Delaware Art Museum
Acquisition Fund, 1983

16. Ellen M. Ingraham (1832–1917)
Out of Work, n.d.
Oil on canvas
30 × 24 3/4 inches
Indianapolis Museum of Art
Gift of Miss Lena L. Ingraham, 23.79

17. George Inness (1825–1894)
The Old Veteran, ca. 1881
Oil on canvas
38 1/2 × 25 1/4 inches
Montclair Art Museum, Montclair, New Jersey
Gift of Mrs. Daniel J. Schuyler, 1953.70

18. Eastman Johnson (1824–1906)
The Pension Claim Agent, 1867
Oil on canvas
25 1/4 × 37 3/8 inches
Fine Arts Museums of San Francisco
Museum purchase, Mildred Anna Williams Collection, 1943.6
HUNTINGTON ONLY

19. Alfred Kappes (1850–1894)
Tattered and Torn, 1886
Oil on canvas
40 × 32 inches
Smith College Museum of Art, Northampton, Massachusetts
Purchased with the Beatrice Oenslager Chace, class of 1928, Fund, the Rita Rich Fraad, class of 1937, Fund for American Art, the Kathleen Compton Sherrerd, class of 1954, Fund for American Art, and with restricted acquisition funds

20. Charles Knoll (life dates unconfirmed)
Panic of 1869, 1869
Oil on canvas
34½ × 27¼ inches
Colby College Museum of Art, Waterville, Maine
Gift of Mr. and Mrs. Ellerton M. Jetté

21. Gustave Kruell (1843–1907)
After Alfred Kappes (American, 1850–1894)
Rent Day, 1887
Engraving
15½ × 12¼ inches
From William MacKay Laffan, Engravings on Wood, by Members of the Society of American Engravers (New York: Harper & Brothers, 1887)
The Huntington Library, Art Collections, and Botanical Gardens, San Marino, California

22. John Harrison Mills (1842–1916)
Artist Painting a Satirical Painting, ca. 1870s–1880s
Oil on canvas
20 × 24½ inches
Collection of Jean and Alvin Snowiss

23. Louis Moeller (1855–1930)
Sign Here, ca. 1890s
Oil on canvas
30 × 40 inches
Collection of Spanierman Gallery, LLC

24. Louis Moeller (1855–1930)
The Will, ca. 1896
Oil on canvas
18 × 24 inches
Garzoli Gallery, San Rafael, California

25. Hal Alexander Courtney Morrison (ca. 1850–1927)
Weighing the Cotton, 1885–90
Oil on canvas
31½ × 45½ inches
Morris Museum of Art, Augusta, Georgia, 1989.01.123
PALMER MUSEUM OF ART ONLY

26. Henry Mosler (1841–1920)
The Fair Exchange, 1881
Oil on canvas
35 × 28 inches
Cincinnati Art Museum
Gift of The Procter & Gamble Company, 2003.88

27. Frank Moss (1838–1924)
A Difficult Job, n.d.
Oil on walnut panel
8⅝ × 7⅛ inches
The State Museum of Pennsylvania, Harrisburg
Transfer from Hope Lodge, 75.1

28. William Sidney Mount (1807–1868)
Fair Exchange, No Robbery, 1865
Oil on panel
26 × 33½ inches
The Long Island Museum of American Art, History & Carriages, Stony Brook, New York
Gift of Mr. and Mrs. Ward Melville

29. Albert Pinkham Ryder (1847–1917)
The Poor Artist, n.d.
Oil on canvas
7¹⁄₁₆ × 12 inches
Princeton University Art Museum
Gift of Alastair B. Martin, Class of 1938, y1957-11

30. Alice Barber Stephens (1858–1932)
The Woman in Business, 1897
Oil on canvas
25 × 18 inches
Brandywine River Museum, Chadds Ford, Pennsylvania
Museum Purchase, 1982, acquisition made possible through Ray and Beverly Sacks
PALMER MUSEUM OF ART ONLY

31. Julian Alden Weir (1852–1919)
The Flower Seller, ca. 1879
Oil on canvas
40⅜ × 22⅛ inches
Brooklyn Museum
Gift of George A. Hearn, 11.522

32. James McNeill Whistler (1834–1903)
Beggars, ca. 1892
Etching with drypoint on off-white paper
$11\frac{15}{16} \times 8\frac{5}{16}$ inches
Terra Foundation for American Art, Chicago
Daniel J. Terra Collection, 1994.8

33. James McNeill Whistler (1834–1903)
A Chelsea Shop, 1894–95
Oil on panel
$5 \times 8\frac{7}{16}$ inches
Terra Foundation for American Art, Chicago
Daniel J. Terra Collection, 1992.148

34. James McNeill Whistler (1834–1903)
Rose and Red: The Barber's Shop, Lyme Regis, 1895
Oil on wood panel
$4\frac{7}{8} \times 8\frac{1}{4}$ inches
Georgia Museum of Art, University of Georgia, Eva Underhill Holbrook Memorial Collection of American Art, Gift of Alfred H. Holbrook, GMOA 1945.96
PALMER MUSEUM OF ART ONLY

35. James McNeill Whistler (1824–1903)
La Marchande de Moutarde, 1858
Etching
$6\frac{1}{8} \times 3\frac{3}{8}$ inches
Palmer Museum of Art, The Pennsylvania State University
Gift of Bertil E. Lofstrom, Class of 1954, 97.10

36. Thomas Waterman Wood (1823–1903)
Crossing the Ferry, 1878
Watercolor
$18\frac{3}{4} \times 26\frac{1}{4}$ inches
T. W. Wood Gallery and Arts Center, Montpelier, Vermont

37. Thomas Waterman Wood (1823–1903)
The Yankee Pedlar, 1872
Oil on canvas
28×40 inches
Terra Foundation for American Art, Chicago
Daniel J. Terra Art Acquisition Endowment Fund, 1998.3

Selected Bibliography

"Albert Bierstadt's Schedules." *New York Times*, February 14, 1895, p. 4.

Beckwith, J. Carroll. Papers. Archives of American Art, Smithsonian Institution, Washington D.C. Reel 800.

Blaugrund, Annette. *The Tenth Street Studio Building: Artist-Entrepreneurs from the Hudson River School to the American Impressionists*. Seattle: University of Washington Press, 1997.

Bolger, Doreen et al., eds. *William M. Harnett*. New York: Harry N. Abrams for the Amon Carter Museum of Art and the Metropolitan Museum of Art, 1992.

Broun, Elizabeth. *Albert Pinkham Ryder*. Washington, D.C.: Smithsonian Institution Press, 1989.

Brownlee, W. Elliot. *Federal Taxation in America: A Short History*. New York: Cambridge University Press, 1996.

Burns, Sarah. *Inventing the Modern Artist: Art and Culture in Gilded Age America*. New Haven: Yale University Press, 1996.

________. *Painting the Dark Side: Art and the Gothic Imagination in Nineteenth-Century America*. Berkeley: University of California Press, 2004.

________. *Pastoral Inventions: Rural Life in Nineteenth-Century American Art and Culture*. Philadelphia: Temple University Press, 1989.

Catalogue of the Private Art Collection of Thomas B. Clarke, New York ... New York: American Art Association, 1899.

Chambers, Bruce. *The World of David Gilmour Blythe*. Washington, D.C.: National Collection of Fine Arts and Smithsonian Institution Press, 1980.

Chandler, Alfred D. *The Visible Hand: The Managerial Revolution in American Business*. Cambridge, Mass.: Belknap Press of Harvard University Press, 1977.

Colbert, Charles. "*Fair Exchange No Robbery*: William Sidney Mount's Commentary on Modern Times." *American Art* 8 (Summer–Autumn 1994): 29–41.

Curry, David Park. *James McNeill Whistler: Uneasy Pieces*. Richmond: Virginia Museum of Fine Arts, 2004.

Foner, Eric. *Reconstruction: America's Unfinished Revolution*, 1863–1877. New York: Harper & Row, 1988.

George, Henry. *Progress and Poverty: An Inquiry into the Cause of Industrial Depressions, and of Increase of Want with Increase of Wealth*... 1879; New York: D. Appleton and Company, 1880.

Gerdts, William C. *Louis Moeller, N.A. (1855–1930): A Victorian Man's World*. New York: Grand Central Art Galleries, 1984.

Gilbert, Barbara C. *Henry Mosler Rediscovered: A Nineteenth-Century American-Jewish Artist*. Los Angeles: Skirball Museum/Skirball Cultural Center, 1995.

Goodwyn, Lawrence. *Democratic Promise: The Populist Movement in America*. New York: Oxford University Press, 1976.

Grieve, Alastair. "The Sites of Whistler's Venice Etchings." *Print Quarterly* 13 (March 1996): 20–39.

Hills, Patricia. *The Painters' America: Rural and Urban Life, 1810–1910*. New York: Praeger, 1974.

Homer, William I. "A Group of Paintings and Drawings by Ryder." *Record of the Art Museum, Princeton University* 18, no. 1 (1959): 17–33.

Hoppin, Martha J. *Country Paths and City Sidewalks: The Art of John George Brown*. Springfield, Mass.: George Walter Vincent Smith Art Museum, 1989.

Hull, David Stewart. *James Henry Cafferty*. New York: New-York Historical Society, 1986.

Husch, Gail E. "*Poor White Folks and Western Squatters*: James Henry Beard's Images of Emigration." *American Art* 7 (Summer 1993): 15–38.

Johns, Elizabeth. *American Genre Painting: The Politics of Everyday Life*. New Haven: Yale University Press, 1991.

Katz, Wendy J. "Fancy Painting, Street Children and the Fast Men of the Pavé." *Nineteenth-Century Studies* 21 (2007): 85–126.

Lansing, Amy Kurtz. *Historical Fictions: Edward Lamson Henry's Paintings of Past and Present*. New Haven: Yale University Art Gallery, 2005.

Lears, Jackson. *No Place of Grace: Antimodernism and the Transformation of American Culture, 1880–1920*. New York: Pantheon, 1981.

________. *Rebirth of a Nation: The Making of Modern America, 1877–1920*. New York: Harper, 2009.

Logue, Larry M., and Michael Barton, eds. *The Civil War Veteran: A Historical Reader*. New York: New York University Press, 2007.

Mazow, Leo G. "George Inness, Henry George, the Single Tax, and the Future Poet." *American Art* 18 (Spring 2004): 58–77.

Moreland, Kim. *The Medievalist Impulse in American Literature: Twain, Adams, Fitzgerald, and Hemingway*. Charlottesville: University Press of Virginia, 1996.

Morgan, Jo-Ann. "Selling the Old South for the New Century." *American Art* 9, no. 1 (1995): 86–109.

Murphy, Kevin M. "Economics of Style: The Business Practices of American Artists and the Structure of the Market 1850–1910." PhD diss., University of California, Santa Barbara, 2005.

________. "Painting for Money: Winslow Homer as Entrepreneur." *Winterthur Portfolio* 37 (Summer/Autumn 2002): 147–60.

O'Leary, Elizabeth L. *At Beck and Call: The Representation of Domestic Servants in Nineteenth-Century American Painting*. Washington, D.C.: Smithsonian Institution Press, 1996.

Orcutt, Kimberly. "Buy American? The Debate Over the Art Tariff." *American Art* 16 (Fall 2002): 82–91.

Ott, John. "How New York Stole the Luxury Art Market: Blockbuster Auctions and Bourgeois Identity in Gilded Age America." *Winterthur Portfolio* 42 (Summer/Autumn 2008): 133–58.

Perry, Claire. *Young America: Childhood in 19th-Century Art and Culture*. New Haven: Yale University Press, in association with Iris & Gerald B. Cantor Center for Visual Arts, Stanford University, 2006.

Peters, Lisa N. "Images of the Homeless in American Art, 1860–1910." In *On Being Homeless: Historical Perspectives*, edited by Rick Beard, 42–67. New York: Museum of the City of New York, 1988.

Quick, Michael *George Inness: A Catalogue Raisonné*. 2 vols. New Brunswick, N.J.: Rutgers University Press, 2007.

Rezeneck, Samuel. *Business Depressions and Financial Panics: Essays in American Business and Economic History*. New York: Greenwood, 1968.

Rodgers, Daniel T. *The Work Ethic in Industrial America, 1850–1920*. Chicago: University of Chicago Press, 1978.

Skalet, Linda Henefield. "The Market for American Painting in New York: 1870-1915." PhD diss., Johns Hopkins University, 1980

Sobel, Robert. *Panic on Wall Street: A Classic History of America's Financial Disasters*. Washington, D.C.: Beard Books, 1999.

Trachtenberg, Alan. *The Incorporation of America: Culture and Society in the Gilded Age*. New York: Hill and Wang, 1982.

Weinberg, H. Barbara. "Thomas B. Clarke, Foremost Patron of American Art from 1872 to 1899." *American Art Journal* 8 (May 1976): 52–83.

Weinberg, H. Barbara, and Carrie Rebora Barratt, eds. *American Stories: Paintings of Everyday Life, 1765–1915*. New York: Metropolitan Museum of Art, 2009.

Williams, Hermann Warner. *Mirror to the American Past: A Survey of American Genre Painting: 1750–1900*. New York: New York Graphic Society, 1973.
Wood, Charles Erskine Scott. Papers. The Huntington Library, Art Collections, and Botanical Gardens, San Marino, California.
Zelizer, Viviana A. *The Social Meaning of Money: Pin Money, Paycheck, Poor Relief, and Other Currencies*. New York: Basic Books, 1994.